ALSO BY JULIO CORTÁZAR

THE WINNERS

HOPSCOTCH

END OF THE GAME

62: A MODEL KIT

ALL FIRES THE FIRE AND OTHER STORIES

A MANUAL FOR MANUEL

Cronopios and Famas

CRONOPIOS
AND
FAMAS

BY JULIO CORTÁZAR Translated
from the Spanish by PAUL BLACKBURN
PANTHEON BOOKS *A Division of Random House, New York*

Library of Congress Catalog Card Number: 69–15477
ISBN: 0-394-73616-8

Manufactured in the United States of America

Designed by Kenneth Miyamoto

FIRST PANTHEON PAPERBACK EDITION

THIS BOOK
CONTAINS THE FOLLOWING ASSORTMENT:

THE INSTRUCTION
MANUAL

The job of having to soften up the brick every day, the job of cleaving a passage through the glutinous mass that declares itself to be the world, to collide every morning with the same narrow rectangular space with the disgusting name, filled with doggy satisfaction that everything is probably in its place, the same woman beside you, the same shoes, the same taste of the same toothpaste, the same sad houses across the street, the filthy slats on the shutters with the inscription THE HOTEL BELGIUM.

Drive the head like a reluctant bull through the transparent mass at the center of which we take a coffee with milk and open the newspaper to find out what has happened in whatever corner of that glass brick. Go ahead, deny up and down that the delicate act of turning the doorknob, that act which may transform everything, is done with the indifferent vigor of a daily reflex. See you later, sweetheart. Have a good day.

Tighten your fingers around a teaspoon, feel its metal pulse, its mistrustful warning. How it hurts to refuse a spoon, to say no to a door, to deny everything that habit has licked to a suitable smoothness. How much simpler to accept the easy request of the spoon, to use it, to stir the coffee.

And it's not that it's so bad that things meet us every day and are the same. That the same woman is there beside us, the same watch, that the novel lying open there on the table starts once more to take its bicycle ride through our glasses. What could be wrong with that? But like a sad bull, one has to lower the head, hustle out from the middle of the glass brick toward the one nearest us, who is as unattainable as the picador, however close the bull is to him. Punish the eyes looking at that which passes in the sky and cunningly accept that its name is cloud, its answer catalogued in the mind. Don't believe that the telephone is going to give you the numbers you try to call, why should it? The only thing that will come is what you have already prepared and decided, the gloomy reflection of your expectations, that monkey, who scratches himself on the table and trembles with cold. Break that monkey's head, take a run from the middle of the room to the wall and break through it. Oh, how they sing upstairs! There's an apartment upstairs in this house with other people in it. A floor upstairs where people live who don't know there's a downstairs floor and that all of us live in the glass brick. And if suddenly a moth lands on the edge of a pencil and flutters there like an ash-colored flame, look at it, I am looking at it, I am touching its tiny heart and I hear it, that moth reverberates in the pie dough of frozen glass, all is not lost. When the door opens and I lean over the stairwell, I'll know that the street begins down there; not the already accepted matrix, not the familiar houses, not the hotel

Julio Cortázar

across the street: the street, that busy wilderness which can tumble upon me like a magnolia any minute, where the faces will come to life when I look at them, when I go just a little bit further, when I smash minutely against the pie dough of the glass brick and stake my life while I press forward step by step to go pick up the newspaper at the corner.

INSTRUCTIONS ON HOW TO CRY

Putting the reasons for crying aside for the moment, we might concentrate on the correct way to cry, which, be it understood, means a weeping that doesn't turn into a big commotion nor proves an affront to the smile with its parallel and dull similarity. The average, everyday weeping consists of a general contraction of the face and a spasmodic sound accompanied by tears and mucus, this last toward the end, since the cry ends at the point when one energetically blows one's nose.

In order to cry, steer the imagination toward yourself, and if this proves impossible owing to having contracted the habit of believing in the exterior world, think of a duck covered with ants or of those gulfs in the Straits of Magellan *into which no one sails ever.*

Coming to the weeping itself, cover the face decorously, using both hands, palms inward. Children are to cry with the sleeve of the dress or shirt pressed against the face, preferably in a corner of the room. Average duration of the cry, three minutes.

Julio Cortázar

INSTRUCTIONS ON HOW TO SING

Begin by breaking all the mirrors in the house, let your arms fall to your side, gaze vacantly at the wall, *forget yourself*. Sing one single note, listen to it from inside. If you hear (but this will happen much later) something like a landscape overwhelmed with dread, bonfires between the rocks with squatting half-naked silhouettes, I think you'll be well on your way, and the same if you hear a river, boats painted yellow and black are coming down it, if you hear the smell of fresh bread, the shadow of a horse.

Afterwards, buy a manual of voice instruction and a dress jacket, and please, don't sing through your nose and leave poor Schumann at peace.

INSTRUCTIONS ON or rather EXAMPLES OF HOW TO BE AFRAID

In a small town in Scotland they sell books with one blank page hidden someplace in the volume. If the reader opens to that page and it's three o'clock in the afternoon, he dies.

In the Piazza Quirinal in Rome, there is one spot, unknown even to the initiated after the nineteenth century, from which, under a full moon, the statues of the Dioscuri can be seen to move, fighting against their horses as they rear back.

At Amalfi, where the seacoast ends, there's a jetty which stretches out into the sea and night. Out beyond the last lighthouse, you can hear a dog bark.

A man is squeezing toothpaste onto his brush, all of a sudden he sees the tiny figure of a woman lying on her back, coral sort of, or a breadcrumb that's been painted.

Opening the door of the wardrobe to take out a shirt, an old almanac falls out which comes apart immediately, pages falling out and crumbling, and covers the white linen with millions of dirty paper butterflies.

Julio Cortázar

There was a story about this traveling salesman whose left wrist began to hurt him, just under his wrist watch. When he removed the watch, blood spurted out. The wound showed the imprints of very tiny teeth.

The doctor finishes his examination and his conclusions are very reassuring to us. His cordial and somber voice precedes the medicines, prescriptions for which he is writing out at the moment, seated behind his desk. Every once in a while he raises his head and smiles, to cheer us up. We don't have a thing to worry about, we'll be better inside of a week. We sit at ease in our easy chair, happy, and look idly and distractedly about the room. In the shadowed area beneath the desk, suddenly we see the doctor's legs. The trousers are pulled up to just above the knees and he's wearing women's stockings.

INSTRUCTIONS
ON HOW TO UNDERSTAND THREE
FAMOUS PAINTINGS

Sacred Love and Profane Love
by Titian

This hateful painting depicts a wake on the banks of the Jordan. In only a very few instances has the obtuseness of a painter been able to refer more contemptibly to mankind's hope for a Messiah *who is radiant by his absence;* missing from the canvas which is the world, he shines horribly in the obscene yawn of the marble tomb, while the angel commissioned to announce the resurrection of his dreadful executed flesh waits patiently for the signs to be fulfilled. It will be unnecessary to explain that the angel is the nude figure prostituting herself in her marvelous plumpness, and disguised as Mary Magdalen, mockery of mockeries, at the moment when the true Mary Magdalen is coming along the road (where, on the other hand, swells the venomous blasphemy of two rabbits).

The child putting his hand into the tomb is Luther, or maybe the Devil. Of the clothed figure it has been said that she represents Glory about to announce that all human ambition fits into a washbowl; but she's badly painted and reminds one of artificial flowers or a lightning flash like a soft sponge-rubber baseball bat.

Julio Cortázar

Lady of the Unicorn
by Raphael

Saint-Simon thought he saw in this portrait a confession of heresy. The unicorn, the narwhal, the obscene pearl in the locket that pretends to be a pear, and the gaze of Maddalena Strozzi fixed dreadfully upon a point where lascivious poses or a flagellation scene might be taking place: here Raphael Sanzio lied his most terrible truth.

The passionate green color in the face of the figure was frequently attributed to gangrene or to the *spring solstice*. The unicorn, a phallic animal, would have infected her: in her body rest all the sins of the world. Then they realized that they had only to remove the overlayers painted by three irritated enemies of Raphael: Carlos Hog, Vincent Grosjean (known as "The Marble"), and Rubens the Elder. The first overpainting was green, the second green, and the third white. It is not difficult to observe here the triple symbol of the deadly nightmoth; the wings conjoined to its dead body they confused with the rose leaves. How often Maddalena Strozzi cut a white rose and felt it squeak between her fingers, twisting and moaning weakly like a tiny mandrake or one of those lizards that sing like lyres when you show them a mirror. But it was already too late and the deadly nightmoth had pricked her. Raphael knew it and sensed she was dying. To paint her truly, then, he added the unicorn, symbol of chastity who will take water from a virgin's hand, sheep and narwhal at once. But he painted the deadly nightmoth in her image, and the unicorn kills his mistress, digs into her superb breast its horn working with lust; it reiterates the process of all principles. What this woman holds in her hands is the mysterious cup from which we have all drunk unknowingly, thirst that we have slaked with other mouths, that red and foamy wine from which come the stars, the worms, and railroad stations.

Portrait of Henry VIII of England
by Holbein

In this canvas people have wanted to see an elephant hunt, a map of Russia, the constellation Lyra, a portrait of the Pope disguised as Henry VIII, a storm over the Sargasso Sea, or the golden polyp which thrives in the latitudes south of Java and which, under the influence of lemon, sneezes delicately and succumbs with a tiny whiff.

Each of these interpretations takes exact account of the general configurations of the painting, whether they are seen from the position in which it is hung or head downwards or held sideways. The differences can be narrowed to the details; the center remains which is GOLD, the number SEVEN, the OYSTER observable in the hat-and-string-tie sections, with the PEARL-head (center irradiating from the pearls on the jacket or central territory) and the general SHOUT absolutely green which bursts forth from the aggregate whole.

Experience simply going to Rome and laying your hand against the king's heart, and you understand the origin of the sea. Even less difficult is to approach it with a lit candle held at the level of the eyes; it will then be seen that *that is not a face* and that the moon, blinded by simultaneity, races across a background of Catherine wheels and tiny transparent ball bearings decapitated in the remembrances in hagiographies. He is not mistaken who sees in this stormy petrifaction a combat between leopards. But also there are reluctant ivory daggers, pages who languish from boredom in long galleries, and a tortuous dialogue between leprosy and the halberds. The man's kingdom is a page out of the great chronicle, but he does not know this and toys peevishly with gloves and fawns. This man looking at you comes back from hell; step away from the canvas and you will see him smile a bit at a time, because he is empty, he is a wind-bag, dry hands hold him up from behind; like a playing-card figure, when you begin to pick him up the castle and everything totters. And his maxim is this: "There is no third dimension, the earth is flat and man drags his belly on the earth. Hallelujah!" It might be the Devil who is saying these words, and maybe you believe them because they are spoken to you by a king.

INSTRUCTIONS ON HOW
TO COMB THE HAIR

There's something like a bone wing from which extends a series of parallels, and the comb isn't the bone but the gaps which penetrate space. The tresses will enter and leave this comb of air with a firm melody, a set design. The lavish play of disarray goes on toward sleep, toward love, toward the wind in the streets, toward rain. Medusa's serpents grow above a superbly handsome face. Comb of swords, a terrifying harvest! But turtle-shell as well, when it's Faustina, bronze gone green for the daughters of Knossos, ivory for Sakuntala, baby-bone for Melisande. Plows furrowing the centuries whose crop will be a perfume, a lariat, a crown; like rolling triremes, those combs of the sea.

So. The man will comb his hair without a mirror, working his open hand through it. The woman will make her reflection into a tower or treetop, whatever peak, where the lines of storm and the blue mark of the broody kingfisher can be found. She'll know how to stem sweetly that flow from tenuous high tides, how to light the fire of remembrance without smoke. To comb the hair will be to take auguries for the rising day, give shape to the lover's secret thought, instruct from the blood the son not yet born.

When it comes to children, let the air comb them.

INSTRUCTIONS ON HOW TO
DISSECT A GROUND OWL

Small ground owls range themselves on posts along the
road
Little old lady ground owls, like wisdom, come out of the
sea
Small young ground owls are like the weather! there it
comes, there it comes
No one stuffs a small owl without a red lantern
Without a red robe in a black room
Without a wardrobe where scratchy wreaths screak
mildly

In the Argentine countryside the little owls await the
hour
Like the Creoles and the Indians they wait without hope
Ranged on posts along the road watching the cars pass
A Buick   a Ford   a Pontiac   a Plymouth   a Cadillac
In which the taxidermists ride with their wives and
children
Without a red robe in a black room
Without a wardrobe where scratchy wreaths screak
mildly

Julio Cortázar

No one stuffs an owl without a red lantern
Without a red robe in a black room

To dissect lions
You need lightning
For little owls you need
Forget-
          fulness.

INSTRUCTIONS ON HOW TO
KILL ANTS IN ROME

Ants, it is said, will eat Rome. They scurry between the flagstones: O she-wolf, what highway of precious stones slices your throat? On every side waters flow from the fountains, the living slate, the tremulous cameos that mumble history, dynasties, and commemorations in the dead of night. One would have to find the heart that makes the fountains leap in order to stave off the ants, and in this city of swollen blood bristling with cornucopias like a blind man's hands, organize a salvation ritual so that the future file down its teeth on the mountains, drag itself off gently and weakly, completely without ants.

First we shall prospect for the sites of the fountains, which is simple, because on the colored maps the fountains also have jets and cascades in sky blue, you only have to locate them precisely and put a circle around them with a blue pencil, not a red one, for a good map of Rome is red as Rome is red. The blue pencil on Rome's red will mark a violet circle around every fountain, and now we are sure we have all of them and that we know the foliage of the waters.

Julio Cortázar

More difficult, more withdrawn and concealed, is the business of drilling through the dark stone under which the veins of mercury run, to take into account by dint of patience the code of all the fountains, and to keep a loving vigil near the imperial vessels on nights when the moon is bright, until after so much green murmuring, so much quavering like flowers, the directions begin to come clear, the confluences, *the other streets*, the living ones. And to track them down without sleeping, with hazel rods shaped in a fork, triangular, with two verges in each hand, one held only loosely between the fingers, but all this invisible to the carabinieri and the amicably suspicious population: go by way of the Quirinal, climb to the Campidoglio, run shouting through the Pincio, land with a motionless apparition like a ball of fire on the orderly walks of the Piazza della Essedra, this is how to extract from the ground's silent metals the catalogue of subterranean rivers. And ask help of no one. Ever.

Afterwards, you will see it gradually, how, in this flayed marble hand, the veins wander leisurely and sonorous, for the pleasure of the waters, for the artifice of the play, until coming closer little by little, they join in the confluence, interweave, swell into arteries, spill out their continuities into the central square where the drum of liquid glass throbs, the root of the pale crowns of trees, the abstruse horse. And then we shall know where it is, in which water table of calcified vaults, between the minuscule skeletons of lemurs, the heart of the water hammers out its time.

It takes some trouble to find out, but it will be found out. Then we'll kill the ants that lust after the fountains, we'll burn out the tunnels these monstrous miners have devised in order to draw close to the secret life of Rome. We shall kill the ants by arriving before them at the central fountain. And we'll leave by the night train fleeing the vengeful demons, vaguely happy, hobnobbing with soldiers and nuns.

INSTRUCTIONS ON HOW
TO CLIMB A STAIRCASE

No one will have failed to observe that frequently the floor bends in such a way that one part rises at a right angle to the plane formed by the floor and then the following section arranges itself parallel to the flatness, so as to provide a step to a new perpendicular, a process which is repeated in a spiral or in a broken line to highly variable elevations. Ducking down and placing the left hand on one of the vertical parts and the right hand upon the corresponding horizontal, one is in momentary possession of a step or stair. Each one of these steps, formed as we have seen by two elements, is situated somewhat higher and further than the one prior, a principle which gives the idea of a staircase, while whatever other combination, producing perhaps more beautiful or picturesque shapes, would be incapable of translating one from the ground floor to the first floor.

You tackle a stairway face on, for if you try it backwards or sideways, it ends up being particularly uncomfortable. The natural stance consists of holding oneself upright, arms hanging easily at the sides, head erect but not so much so that the eyes no longer see the steps immediately above, while one tramps up, breathing lightly and with regularity. To climb a staircase one begins by lifting that part of the body located below and to the right, usually encased in leather or deerskin, and which, with a few exceptions, fits exactly on the stair. Said part set down on the first step (to abbreviate we shall call it "the foot"), one draws up the equivalent part on the left side (also called "foot" but not to be confused with "the foot" cited above), and lifting this other part to the level of "the foot," makes it continue along until it is set in place on the second step, at which point the foot will rest, and "the foot" will rest on the first. (The first steps are always the most difficult, until you acquire the necessary coordination. The coincidence of names between the foot and "the foot" makes the explanation more difficult. Be especially careful not to raise, at the same time, the foot and "the foot.")

Having arrived by this method at the second step, it's easy enough to repeat the movements alternately, until one reaches the top of the staircase. One gets off it easily, with a light tap of the heel to fix it in place, to make sure it will not move until one is ready to come down.

PREAMBLE TO THE INSTRUCTIONS
ON HOW TO WIND A WATCH

Think of this: When they present you with a watch they are gifting you with a tiny flowering hell, a wreath of roses, a dungeon of air. They aren't simply wishing the watch on you, and many more, and we hope it will last you, it's a good brand, Swiss, seventeen rubies; they aren't just giving you this minute stonecutter which will bind you by the wrist and walk along with you. They are giving you—they don't know it, it's terrible that they don't know it—they are gifting you with a new, fragile, and precarious piece of yourself, something that's yours but not a part of your body, that you have to strap to your body like your belt, like a tiny, furious bit of something hanging onto your wrist. They gift you with the job of having to wind it every day, an obligation to wind it, so that it goes on being a watch; they gift you with the obsession of looking into jewelry-shop windows to check the exact time, check the radio announcer, check the telephone service. They give you the gift of fear, someone will steal it from you, it'll fall on the street and get broken. They give you the gift of your trademark and the assurance that it's a trademark better than the others, they gift you with the impulse to compare your watch with other watches. They aren't giving you a watch, you are the gift, they're giving you yourself for the watch's birthday.

INSTRUCTIONS ON HOW
TO WIND A WATCH

Death stands there in the background, but don't be afraid. Hold the watch down with one hand, take the stem in two fingers, and rotate it smoothly. Now another installment of time opens, trees spread their leaves, boats run races, like a fan time continues filling with itself, and from that burgeon the air, the breezes of earth, the shadow of a woman, the sweet smell of bread.

What did you expect, what more do you want? Quickly strap it to your wrist, let it tick away in freedom, imitate it greedily. Fear will rust all the rubies, everything that could happen to it and was forgotten is about to corrode the watch's veins, cankering the cold blood and its tiny rubies. And death is there in the background, we must run to arrive beforehand and understand it's already unimportant.

UNUSUAL
OCCUPATIONS

SIMULACRA

We are an uncommon family. In this country where things are done only to boast of them or from a sense of obligation, we like independent occupations, jobs that exist just because, simulacra which are completely useless.

We have one failing: we lack originality. Nearly everything we decide to do is inspired by—let's speak frankly, is copied from—celebrated examples. If we manage to contribute any innovation whatsoever, it always proves to have been inevitable: anachronisms, or surprises, or scandals. My elder uncle says that we're like carbon copies, identical with the original except another color, another paper, another end product. My third-youngest sister compares herself to Andersen's mechanical nightingale. Her romanticizing is disgusting.

There are a lot of us and we live in Humboldt Street.

We do things, but it's difficult to tell about it because the most important elements are missing: the anxiety and the expectation of doing the things, the surprises so much more important than the results, the calamities and abortive undertakings where the whole family collapses like a card castle and for whole days you don't hear anything but wailing and peals of laughter. Telling what we do is hardly a way of filling in the inevitable gaps, because sometimes we're poor or in jail or sick, sometimes somebody dies or (it hurts me to mention it) someone goes straight, finks out, renounces us, or heads in the UNPOSITIVE DIRECTION. But there's no reason to conclude from this that things are terrible with us or that we're incurably unhappy. We live in this lower-middle-class neighborhood called the barrio Pacífico, and we do things every chance we get. There are a lot of us who come up with ideas and manage to put them into action. The gallows for instance: up till now, no one's agreed on how the idea got started; my fifth sister asserts that it was one of my first cousins, who are very much philosophers, but my elder uncle insists that it occurred to him after reading a cloak-and-dagger novel. Basically, it's not very important to us, the only thing that counts is to do things, and that's why I tell it, unwillingly almost, only so as not to feel so close the emptiness of this rainy afternoon.

The house has a garden in front of it, an uncommon thing in Humboldt Street. It's not much bigger than a patio, but it's three steps higher than the sidewalk, which gives it the fine aspect of a platform, the ideal site for a gallows. As it has a high railing of ironwork and masonry, one can work without the passers-by being, as one might say, installed in the house itself; they can station themselves at the railings and hang around there

Julio Cortázar

for hours, which doesn't bother us. "We shall begin at the full moon," my father ruled. By day we went to find lengths of wood and iron in the warehouses in the Avenida Juan B. Justo, but my sisters stayed home in the parlor practicing the wolf howl, after my youngest aunt maintained that gallows trees draw wolves and move them to howl at the moon. The responsibility of acquiring a supply of nails and other hardware fell to my cousins; my elder uncle made a sketch of the plans, and discussed with my mother and my other uncle the variety and quality of the various instruments of torture. I remember the end of that discussion: they decided austerely on a reasonably high platform upon which would be constructed the gibbet and a rack and wheel, with an open space which could be used for torture or beheading, depending upon the case. It seemed to my elder uncle a rather poor and meeching construction compared with his original idea, but the size of the front garden and the cost of construction materials are always restricting the family's ambitions.

We began the construction work on a Sunday afternoon after the raviolis. Although we had never concerned ourselves with what the neighbors might think, it was clear that the few onlookers thought we were adding one or two floors to enlarge the house. The first to be astonished was Don Cresta, the little old man in the house across from us, and he came over to inquire why we were putting up a platform like that. My sisters were gathered in one corner of the garden and were letting loose with a few wolf howls. A goodly group of people gathered, but we went on working until nightfall and got the platform finished and the two little sets of stairs (for the priest and the condemned man, who ought not to go up together). Monday one part of the family went to its respective employments and occupations, after all, you have to live somehow, and the rest of us began to put up the gibbet while my elder uncle consulted ancient engravings to find a model for the rack and wheel. His idea was to set the wheel as high as possible upon a slightly irregular pole, for example a well-trimmed poplar trunk. To humor him, my second-oldest brother and my first cousins went off with the pickup truck to find a poplar; my elder uncle and my mother, meanwhile, were fitting the spokes of the wheel into the hub and I was getting an iron collar ready. In those moments we amused ourselves enormously because you could hear hammering on all sides, my sisters howling in the parlor, the neighbors crowding against the iron railings exchanging impressions, and the silhouette of the gibbet rose between the rosaniline bed and the evening mallows and you could see my younger uncle astride the crosspiece driving in the hook and fixing the running knot for the noose.

At this stage of things the people in the street could not help realizing what it was we were building, and a chorus of threats and protests was an agreeable encouragement to put the final stroke to the day's labor by erecting the wheel. Several disorderly types had made an effort to keep my second-oldest brother and my cousins from conveying into the house the magnificent poplar trunk which they'd fetched in the pickup truck. An attempt at harassment in the form of a tug of war was

Julio Cortázar

won easily by the family in full force tugging at the trunk in a disciplined way, and we set it down in the garden along with a very young child trapped in the roots. My father personally returned the child to its exasperated parents, putting it genteelly through the railings, and while attention was concentrated on these sentimental alternatives, my elder uncle aided by my first cousins fitted the wheel onto one end of the trunk and proceeded to raise it. The family was congregated on the platform at the moment the police arrived and commented favorably on how well the gallows looked. My third sister had stationed herself alone by the gate, so the dialogue with the deputy commissioner himself was left up to her; it was not difficult for her to persuade him that we were laboring within the precincts of our own property upon a project only the use of which could vest it with an illegal character, and that the complaints of the neighborhood were the products of animosity and the result of envy. Nightfall saved us from losing any more time.

We took supper on the platform by the light of a carbide lamp, spied upon by a crowd of around a hundred spiteful neighbors; never had the roast suckling pig tasted more exquisite, or the chianti been blacker and sweeter. A breeze from the north swung the gallows rope gently back and forth; the wheel of the rack creaked once or twice, as though the crows had already come to rest there and eat. The spectators began to go off, muttering vague threats; some twenty or thirty stayed on, hanging around the iron railing—they seemed to be waiting for something. After coffee we put out the lamp so that we could see the moon, which was rising over the balustrades of the terrace, my sisters howled, and my cousins and uncles loped slowly back and forth across the platform, their steps making the foundation shake underfoot. In the subsequent silence the moonlight came to fall at the height of the noose, and a cloud with silver borders seemed to stretch across the wheel. We looked at it all, so happy it was a pleasure, but the neighbors were murmuring at the railings as if they were disappointed or something. They were lighting cigarettes or were wandering off, some in pajamas and others more slowly. Only the street remained, the sound of the cop's nightstick on pavement in the distance, and the 108 bus which passed every once in a while; as for us, we had already gone to sleep, and were dreaming of fiestas, elephants, and silk suits.

Julio Cortázar

CEREMONY AND PROTOCOL

It has always seemed to me that the distinctive trait of our family is restraint. We carry modesty to incredible extremes, as much in our manner of dressing and of eating as in our way of expressing ourselves or getting onto trams. Nicknames, for example, which in the barrio Pacífico are so unscrupulously assigned, are for us an occasion for care, reflection, even uneasiness. It seems to us that you can't simply attach any old nickname to someone who will have to digest it and tolerate it as a permanent adjunct for the rest of his life. The ladies in Humboldt Street call their sons Toto, Coco, or Tiny, and the girls Brownie or Doll, but this plain variety of nickname does not exist in our family, much less the rarer and terrifying ones such as Scarface, Professor, or Sharkey, which abound around Paraguay and Godoy Cruz. To show you the caution we employ in such matters, one has only to cite the case of my younger aunt. Visibly endowed with a backside of impressive dimensions, yet we would never have permitted ourselves the easy temptation of the customary nicknames; thus, instead of giving her the brutish nickname "Etruscan Amphora" we agreed on the more decent and homely one "Rumpy." We always proceed with the same tact, although it happens that we have fights with the neighbors, who insist upon the traditional devices. Now in the case of my younger second cousin, who carries around a remarkably large head, we always rejected the nickname "Atlas," which had been given to him at the snack bar on the corner, and preferred the infinitely more delicate one "Pinhead"—etcetera.

I should like to make clear that we don't do these things to differentiate ourselves from the rest of the neighborhood. It's only that we should like to modify routines and traditions gradually, and without ruffling anyone's feelings. Vulgarity in any of its forms displeases us, and if, down at the bar, one of us hears phrases like "It was a game with some rough action," or "Faggioli's game was characterized by a good deal of early infiltration down the center line," that's enough for us: we immediately drop our firm adherence to form and good breeding and whip out the locutions most advisable under the emergency circumstances, for instance: "He made one of those kicks I owe you," or "We rapped them around a little, then we really scored." People look at us with surprise, but no one ever misses the lesson concealed in these delicate phrases. My older uncle, who reads the Argentine writers, says that it would be a good idea to work a similar gig with some of their work, but he's never explained this to us in detail. A shame.

POSTAL & TELEGRAPH SERVICE

One time a very distant relative of ours managed to get
to be a minister and we fixed it so that a large part of the
family received appointments in the post office substa-
tion in the calle de Serrano. It didn't last long, that's for
sure. Of the three days we were there, two of them we
spent attending to the needs of the public with astound-
ing celerity, which served us well on a surprise visit by
an inspector from the Central Post Office and earned us
a laudatory squib in the *Civil Service Leader*. We were
certain of our popularity by the third day, for people
were already coming in from other sections of the city to
send off their correspondence and to make out money
orders to Purmamarca and other equally absurd places.
Then my elder uncle gave us free rein and the family
really began handling things, adapting procedures to
their principles and predilections. At the stamp window,
my second-youngest sister was giving away a colored
balloon to everyone who bought stamps. The first re-
cipient of a balloon was a stout housewife, who stood
there as if she'd been nailed to the floor, balloon in one
hand, in the other a one-peso stamp, already licked,

which was curling up on her finger little by little. A youth with long hair flatly refused to accept his balloon, and my sister admonished him severely, while contrary opinions began to be raised in the line behind him. At the next window, divers provincials stupidly engaged in remitting part of their salaries to their distant relatives were somewhat astonished to receive small shots of vodka and every once in a while a breaded veal cutlet; all this my father took charge of, and to top it off he recited the old gaucho Vizcacha's better maxims at the top of his lungs. My brothers, in the meantime, in charge of the parcel-post counter, had smeared the packages with tar and were dunking them in a bucket filled with feathers. They presented them later to the thunderstruck truckman, pointing out the happiness with which such improved packages would be received. "No string showing," they said. "Without all that vulgar sealing wax, and with the name of the addressee that looks like it's been printed under a swan's wing, you notice?" Not everyone proved to be enchanted, one has to be truthful about it.

When the bystanders and the police invaded the premises, my mother closed the act with a beautiful gesture, she flew many paper airplanes over the heads of the assembled public, all different colors, made from telegrams, forms for postal money orders and for registered letters. We sang the national anthem and retired in good order; I saw a little girl, third in line at the stamp window, crying, when she realized it was already too late for them to give her a balloon.

Julio Cortázar

THE LOSS AND RECOVERY OF THE HAIR

In his struggle against pragmatism and the horrible tendency of reaching useful ends, my eldest cousin proposed the following procedure: to pull from the head a good thick strand of hair, make a knot in the middle of it, and drop it gently down the sink drain. Should the hair get trapped in the metal grate which used to propagate in such drains, all you have to do is open the faucet a bit and it will disappear for good.

Without a moment of hesitation, you must begin the job of recovering the hair. The first operation is narrowed down to taking the sink trap apart to see if the hair has got itself hung up in one of the corrugations in the pipe. If you don't find it, you have to begin opening that section of the pipe which runs from the trap via the various conduits to the pipes of the main outlet channel. Now you're dead sure of finding a lot of hairs in this section, and you'll have to count on the rest of the family to help examine them one at a time to find the one with the knot. If it doesn't turn up, one is faced with the interesting problem of breaking open the plumbing all the way to the ground floor, but this entails a major effort, inasmuch as one would have to work eight or ten years in some ministry or business to amass enough money to make it possible to buy the four apartments located under where my eldest cousin lives, all which with the extraordinary disadvantage that while one is working those eight or ten years, there's no way to avoid the aggravating feeling that the strand of hair hasn't yet got to that part of the plumbing, and through some remote chance, has only gotten stuck in some rusty out-jutting of the pipe.

The day comes when we can break open the pipes in all the apartments, and for months we'll live surrounded by washbasins and other containers full of wet hair, as well as hired helpers and beggars, whom we pay generously to seek out, separate, classify, and bring us the possible globs of hair in order to arrive at that absolute certainty so devoutly to be wished. If the hair does not show up, we begin a much vaguer and more complicated stage, because the next stretch brings us to the city's sewer mains. After having purchased a special suit, we'll learn how to creep through the sewer pipes late at night, armed with an immense lantern and oxygen mask, and we shall explore the lesser and the greater galleries, aided if possible by assorted groups of vagrants with whom we will have contracted a working relationship and to whom we shall have to give the larger part of the monies which we earn during the day in a ministry or business office.

Very frequently we shall be under the impression that we've come to the end of the task, since we'll find (or

Julio Cortázar

they'll bring us) a hair that seems to be the one we're looking for; but since one never knows in any single case that a knot has not occurred in the middle of the hair without the intervention of human hands, we nearly always decide by comparison that the questionable knot is a simple swelling in the size of the hair (though we know of no similar occurrence) or a deposit produced by some silicate or whatever oxide during its long residence on a damp surface. By this time it's likely that we have worked our way through the smaller and larger sections of mains to the point at which no one would decide to go further: the main channel headed toward the river, that torrential consolidation of waste products wherein no amount of money, no boat, no hire or bribery will permit us to continue our search.

But before that happens, much earlier perhaps, a few centimeters from the sink drain for example, at the second-floor apartment level, or in the first underground pipes, it might happen that we would find the hair. Just think of the happiness this would give us, just the astonishing realization of the efforts saved by sheer chance, to be able to justify, to choose, practically to insist upon some such project, which every conscientious teacher ought to recommend to his students, even those at the most tender age, instead of parching their souls with the principle of multiplication to the third power, or General Custer's troubles at Little Big Horn.

AUNT WITH DIFFICULTIES

Why do we have to have an aunt who's so afraid of falling on her back? For years the family has struggled to cure her of her obsession, but the time has come to admit our crashing failure. The more we do, the more aunt is afraid to fall on her back; and her innocent mania affects everyone, starting with my father who, in brotherly fashion, escorts her to different parts of the house and maintains a constant reconnaissance of the floor so that aunt may walk about without concern, while my mother sweeps out the patio several times a day, my sisters pick up the tennis balls with which they disport themselves innocently on the terrace, and my cousins wash off every trace ascribable to the dogs, cats, turtles, and hens which proliferate through the house. But nothing works; aunt makes up her mind to pass through rooms only after a long tottering hesitation, interminable observations by eye, and intemperate words to any kid who happens by at the moment. Then she gets under way, favoring one foot first, moving it like a boxer in the resin box, then the other, shifting her body in a displacement which seemed majestic to us in our youth,

Julio Cortázar

and taking several minutes to get from one doorway to another. It's really horrible.

At different times the family has tried to get my aunt to explain with some sort of coherence her fear of falling on her back. On one occasion the attempt was received with a silence you could have cut with a scythe; but one night, after her glass of sweet wine, aunt condescended to imply that if she were to fall on her back she wouldn't be able to get up again. At which elemental observation, thirty-two members of the family swore they would come to her aid; she responded with a weary glance and two words: "Be useless." Days later, my eldest brother called me into the kitchen one night and showed me a cockroach which had fallen on its back under the sink. Without saying a word, we stood and watched its long and useless struggle to right itself, while other cockroaches, prevailing over the intimidation of the light, traveled across the floor and passed by brushing against the one who was lying there on its back waving its legs. We went to bed in a distinctly melancholy mood that night, and for one reason or another no one resumed the questioning; we limited ourselves now to alleviating her fear as much as possible, escorting her everywhere, offering her our arms and buying her dozens of pairs of shoes with gripper soles, and other stabilizing devices. That way life went on, and was not worse than any other life.

AUNT, EXPLAINED OR NOT

Whether or not anyone cares, my four first cousins are addicted to philosophy. They read books, discuss among themselves, and are much admired, from a distance, by the rest of the family, faithful as we are to the principle of not meddling with the predilections of others, indeed favoring and forwarding them insomuch as possible. These boys, who deserve my great respect, have more than once set themselves the problem of my aunt's fearfulness, arriving at conclusions, obscure perhaps, but worth looking at. As usual under such circumstances, my aunt was the one least interested in these deliberations, but dating from that epoch, the family's deference was even more marked. We have accompanied aunt for years now on her wobbly expeditions from the living room to the front patio, from the bedroom to the bath, from the kitchen to the pantry. It never seemed extraordinary to us that she would sleep on her side, and that during the night she would preserve the most absolute immobility, on her right side on even days, the odd ones on her left. In the dining-room and patio chairs, aunt would sit very erect; not for anything would she

Julio Cortázar

ever accept the comfort of a rocker or a Morris chair. The night Sputnik went up, the family stretched out on the patio tiles to observe the satellite, but aunt remained seated, and the next day had an incredibly stiff neck. We were convinced slowly, but by now we're resigned. Our first cousins are a great help to us, for they allude to the question with knowing glances and say things like "She's right." But why? We do not know, and they don't care to explain it to us. As far as I'm concerned, for example, to be on one's back seems extremely comfortable. The whole body is resting on the mattress or on the tiles in the patio, you feel your heels, the calves of your legs, your thighs, the buttocks, the small of the back, the shoulder blades, the arms, and the nape of the neck, which among them share the weight of the body and spread it out, so to speak, against the floor, they come so close and so naturally to that surface, that it draws us down ferociously and seems to want to gobble us up. It's curious that for me to be flat on my back turns out to be the position most natural for me, and at times I'm afraid that aunt's a little horrified by that. I find it perfect, and believe that, deep down, it is the most comfortable. Yes, I really said that: deep down, really deep down, on your back. So much so that I'm a bit afraid, a thing I can't manage to explain. How I would like so very much to be like her, and how I can't.

THE TIGER LODGERS

Long before bringing our idea to the level of actual practice, we knew that the lodging of tigers presented a double problem, sentimental and moral. The first aspect is not so much related to the lodging as to the tiger himself, insomuch as it is not particularly agreeable for these felines to be lodged and they summon all their energies, which are enormous, to resist being lodged. Is it fitting under those circumstances to defy the idiosyncrasy of the above-mentioned animals? But this question leads us directly to the moral level where any act can be the cause, or the effect, splendid or ignominious. At night, in our little house in Humboldt Street, we meditated over our bowls of rice and milk, forgetting to sprinkle the cinnamon and sugar on them. We were not really sure of our ability to lodge a tiger, and it was depressing.

It was decided finally that we would lodge just one for the sole purpose of seeing the mechanism at work in all its complexity; we could always evaluate the results later. I shall not speak here of the problem of coming by the first tiger: a delicate and troublesome job, a race past consulates, drugstores, a complex chain of tickets, airmail letters, and work with the dictionary. One night my cousins came back covered with tincture of iodine: success. We drank so much chianti that my younger sister ended up having to clear the table with a rake. We were much younger in those days. Now that the experiment has yielded known results, I can supply the details of the lodging. The most difficult perhaps would be to describe everything related to the environment, since it requires a room with a minimum of furniture, a thing rather difficult to find in Humboldt Street. The layout is arranged in the center: two crossed planks, a complex of flexible withies, and several earthenware bowls filled with milk and water. To lodge a tiger is really not too difficult; the operation can miscarry, however, and you've got everything to do over again. The real difficulty begins when, already lodged, the tiger recovers his liberty and chooses —in one of the many manners possible—to exercise it. At that stage, known as the intermediate stage, my family's reactions are pretty basic; everything depends on how my sisters behave, on the smartness with which my father manages to get the tiger lodged again, utilizing the natural propensities of the tiger to the maximum. The slightest mistake would be a catastrophe, the fuses burned out, the milk on the floor, the horror of those phosphorescent eyes shining through the utter darkness, warm spurts with every thud of the paw; I resist imagining what would follow since, up till now, we've managed to lodge a tiger without dangerous consequences. The layout, as well as the varying duties all of us must perforce perform, from the tiger down to my second cousins, are seemingly efficient and articulate harmoniously. The fact of lodging a tiger is not in itself important to us, rather that the ceremony be completed to the very end without a mistake. Either the tiger agrees to be lodged, or must be lodged in such a way that its acceptance or refusal is of no consequence. At these moments which one is tempted to call crucial—perhaps because of the two planks, perhaps because it's a mere commonplace expression—the family feels itself possessed by an extraordinary exaltation; my mother does not hide her tears, and my first cousins knit and unknit their fingers convulsively. Lodging a tiger has something of the total encounter, lining oneself up against an absolute; the balance depends upon so little and we pay so high a price, that these brief moments which follow the lodging and which confirm its perfection sweep us away from ourselves, annihilating both tigerness and humanity in a single motionless movement which is a dizziness, respite, and arrival. There's no tiger, no family, no lodging. Impossible to know what there is: a trembling that is not of this flesh, a centered time, a column of contact. And later we all go out to the covered patio, and our aunts bring out the soup as though something were singing or as if we were all at a baptism.

OUR DEMEANOR AT WAKES

We don't go for the anisette, we don't even go because we're expected to. You'll have guessed our reason already: we go because we cannot stand the craftier forms of hypocrisy. My oldest second cousin takes it upon herself to ascertain the nature of the bereavement, and if it is genuine, if the weeping is genuine because to weep is the only thing left to men and women to do between the odors of lilies and coffee, then we stay at home and escort them from afar. At the most, my mother drops in for a few minutes to represent the family; we don't like to superimpose our strange life upon this dialogue with shadow, that would be insolent. But if my cousin's leisurely investigation discloses the merest suspicion that they've set up the machinery of hypocrisy in a covered patio or in the living room, then the family gets into its best duds, waits until the wake is already under way, and goes to present itself, a few at a time, gradually but implacably.

In the barrio Pacífico, affairs are generally held in a patio with flowerpots and radio music. For these occasions, the neighbors agree to turn off their radios and the only things left are the pots of jasmine and the relatives, alternating along the walls. We arrive separately or in pairs, we greet the relatives of the deceased, you can always tell who they are—they begin to cry almost as soon as anyone walks in the door—and go to pay our last respects to the dear departed, convoyed along by some close relative. One or two hours later, the whole family is in the bereaved house, but although the neighbors know us well, we act as if each of us had come on his own account and we hardly speak among ourselves. Our acts are governed by a precise method by which to select conversational partners with whom one chats in the kitchen, under the orange tree, in the bedrooms, in the hallway, and every once in a while one goes out for a smoke in the patio or into the street, or takes a stroll around the block to air political opinions or talk sports. We don't spend too much time sounding out the feelings of the closest relatives, small tumblers of cane liquor, sweet *mate*, and the cigarettes are the bridge to confidences; before midnight arrives we are sure we can move remorselessly. Generally, my younger sister is in charge of the opening skirmish; cleverly placing herself at the foot of the coffin, she covers her eyes with a violet handkerchief and begins to cry, silently at first, but to that incredible point where the handkerchief is sopping wet, then with hiccups and gasping, and finally she sets out upon a terrible attack of wailing which obliges the neighborhood ladies to carry her to the bed prepared for such emergencies where they give her orange water to sniff and console her, meanwhile other ladies from the neighborhood look after the nearby relatives infected by

Julio Cortázar

the crisis. For a while there's a pile-up of folk in the doorway of the room where the loved one lies in state, whispered questions and answers, the neighbors shrugging their shoulders. Exhausted by a force for which they themselves have had to go all out, the relatives diminish their demonstrations of grief, and just at that moment my three girl cousins set off into a weeping without affectation, no loud cries, but so touchingly that the relatives and the neighbors feel envious, they realize that they can't just sit there resting while strangers from the next block are grieving in such a fashion, again they rise to the general lament, again space must be found on beds, fanning old ladies, loosening belts on convulsed little old men. Usually my brothers and I wait for this moment to make our entrance into the viewing room and we place ourselves together about the coffin. Strange as it may seem we really are grief-stricken; we can never listen to our sisters cry but that an infinite dismay fills our breasts and we remember things from childhood, some fields near the Villa Albertina, a tram that cheeped taking the curve at the calle General Rodríguez in Banfield, things like that, always very sad ones. We need only to see the deceased's crossed hands for a flood of tears to demolish us all at once, compelling us to cover our abashed faces, and we are five men who really cry at wakes, while the relatives desperately gather the breath to match us, feeling that, at whatever cost, they have to make it evident that it's their wake, that only they have the right to cry like that in this house. But there are few of them and they're faking (we know that from my oldest second cousin, and it lends us strength). Hiccups and fainting fits accumulate in vain, the closest neighbors back them up with their consolation and considered meditations, it's useless, carrying or leading them off to rest and recuperate so they can throw themselves renewed back into the struggle. Now my father and elder uncle spell us, there's something that commands respect in the grief of these old men who've come from Humboldt Street, five blocks away if you count from the corner, to keep vigil on the one who has passed away. The more coherent neighbors begin to lose their footing, they finally let the relatives drop and go to the kitchen to drink grappa and comment on the state of affairs; some of the relatives, debilitated by an hour and a half of sustained weeping, are sleeping very loudly. We relieve one another in turns, without giving the impression, however, of anything prearranged; before six in the morning we are the acknowledged masters of the wake, the majority of the neighbors have gone back to their houses to sleep, the relations are lying around in different postures and degrees of bloatedness, dawn falls upon the patio. At that hour my aunts are organizing strong refreshments in the kitchen, we drink boiling coffee, we beam at one another passing in the entryway or the bedrooms; we're a bit like ants, going and coming, rubbing antennae as we pass. When the hearse arrives the seating arrangements have already been decided, my sisters lead the relatives to take final leave of the deceased before the closing of the coffin, support them and comfort them, while my girl cousins and my brothers push forward to displace them, cutting short the final farewell, and remain alone with the corpse. Exhausted, wandering around displaced, understanding vaguely but incapable of reacting, the relatives let themselves be led

Julio Cortázar

and dragged, they drink anything brought to their lips and answer the loving solicitude of my sisters and cousins with vague and inconsistent protests. When the time has come to leave and the house is full of relations and friends, an invisible organization, but with no loopholes, decides every movement, the funeral director respects my father's instructions, the removal of the coffin is accomplished according to the suggestions of my elder uncle. At one point or another, relatives arriving at the last moment start a querulous and disorderly attempt to regain possession; the neighbors, convinced that everything is proceeding apace, look at them scandalized and make them be quiet. My parents and my uncles install themselves in the first car, my brothers get into the second, and my girl cousins condescend to take one of the closer relatives in the third, in which they settle themselves wrapped in great black or purple shawls. The rest get into whatever car they can, and there are relatives who find themselves obliged to call a taxi. And if some of them, revived by the morning air and the long ride, plot a reconquest at the cemetery, they're in for bitter disillusion. The coffin has barely arrived at the cemetery gates when my brothers make a circle around the orator picked by the family or friends of the deceased, easily recognizable by his long, sad, funereal, and prepared face and the little roll of paper bulging from his jacket pocket. Reaching out their hands and grabbing him, they soak his lapels with their tears, they clap his shoulders softly with a sound like tapioca pudding, and the orator cannot prevent my youngest uncle from mounting the platform where he opens the speeches with an oration that is the very soul of truth and discretion. It lasts three minutes, it refers solely to the deceased, it marks the limits of his virtues and notes his defects, and there is humanity in every word he says; he is deeply moved, and at times it is difficult for him to quit. He has hardly stepped down when my oldest brother takes to the platform and launches a panegyric on behalf of the neighborhood; meanwhile the neighbor designated to this task tries to get through a crowd of my sisters and cousins who weep buckets and hang onto his vest. An affable but imperious gesture of my father's mobilizes the funeral-parlor personnel; they set the catafalque softly in motion, and the official orators are still standing at the foot of the platform, mashing their speeches in their wet hands. Normally we don't bother to conduct the deceased to the vault or sepulcher, but usually make a half turn and exit all together, commenting on the incidents during the wake. We watch from a distance the relatives running desperately to grab hold of one of the ropes holding the coffin and fighting with the neighbors who have meanwhile taken possession of the ropes and prefer to carry it themselves rather than let the relatives carry it.

UNSTABLE
STUFF

AT THE OFFICE

My faithful secretary is one of those who take their job seriously, down to the last comma, and you realize what that means, crossing up the chain of command, invading others' territories, sticking five fingers into a glass of milk to fish out one poor little hair.

My faithful secretary takes care of, or would like to take care of, everything in my office. We pass the day cheerfully, carrying on a friendly battle for jurisdiction, smilingly we undermine and countermine, there are sallies and retreats, captures and rescues. But she has time for it all, she not only tries to dominate the office, but also, scrupulously, fulfills her duties. Words for example, not a day goes by that she doesn't polish them up, brush them off, she files them in neat orderliness, grooms and readies them for their daily functions. Should an expendable adjective pop out of my mouth—all those occur outside my secretary's orbit, and in a certain way outside my own—there she is, pencil in hand to trap and kill it, not even leaving it time to weld itself to the rest of the sentence and, through sloppy habit or neglect, survive. If

I left her alone, if at this very moment I left her to her own devices, she'd crumple these papers in rage and throw them in the basket. She is so strongly resolved that I live an orderly life that any unforeseen move moves her to sit up, all ears, tail and nose at point, trembling like a sheep bell in the wind. I have to fake it, and under the pretext that I am editing a report, fill a few sheets of pink or green paper with words which happen to please me with their games and their skipping around and their furious wrangling. My faithful secretary, meanwhile, straightens up the office, apparently distracted, but ready to hop to it. In the middle of a verse which was contentedly coming into being, I hear her begin her horrible squeak of disapproval, then my pencil breaks into a gallop to reach the forbidden words, she erases them promptly, orders the disorder, cuts, cleans it up, makes it resplendent, and what's left is probably fine, but this sadness, this taste of treachery on the tongue, the expression of a boss face to face with his secretary.

Julio Cortázar

MARVELOUS PURSUITS

What a wonderful pursuit: cut the leg off a spider, put it in an envelope, write on it *Minister of Foreign Affairs,* add the address, run downstairs, and drop the letter into the mailbox at the corner.

What a wonderful pursuit: walk down the boulevard Arago counting the trees, and every five chestnut trees stand for a moment on one leg and wait for someone to look, then give a short, tight yell, spin like a top, arms wide, very like the *cakuy* bird who laments in the trees of northern Argentina.

What a wonderful pursuit: go into a café and ask for sugar, again for sugar, three or four times for sugar, continue with great concentration constructing a mountain of sugar, center of the table, while indignation swells along the counters and beneath the white aprons, and then spit, softly, right in the middle of the mountain, and watch the descent of the small glacier of saliva, hear the roar of broken rocks which accompanies it, arising from the contracted throats of five local customers and the boss, an honest man when he feels like it.

What a marvelous pursuit: take the bus, get off in front of the Ministry, hack your way through quickly using an official-looking envelope with heavy seals, leave the last secretary behind, and then seriously and without flinching enter the great office with mirrors, exactly at the moment that an usher in a blue uniform is delivering a letter to the Minister, watch him slit the envelope with a letter opener of historic origin, insert two fingers delicately and come out with the spider's leg and stand there looking at it, then imitate a fly's buzzing and watch how the Minister grows pale, he wants to get rid of the leg but he can't, he's trapped by the leg, turn your back and leave whistling, announce down the corridors that the Minister is resigning, and you realize that the next day enemy troops are entering the city and everything will go to hell, and it'll be a Thursday of an odd-numbered month in leap year.

Julio Cortázar

VIETATO INTRODURRE BICICLETTE
(BICYCLES PROHIBITED)

In the banks and business offices of this world no one gives a hang if someone walks in with a cabbage under his arm, or a toucan, or with the songs my mother taught me spouting from his mouth like a hemp cord, or holding a chimpanzee in a striped T-shirt by the hand. But let someone walk in with a bicycle, what a fuss they raise, the vehicle is ejected forcibly into the street while its hapless owner is subjected to the vehement admonitions of the employees.

For a bicycle, a docile being of modest conduct, it is a humiliation and a mockery to always find these supercilious notices which keep it waiting outside the beautiful glass doors of the city. Be it understood that bicycles have tried every means to better their dismal social condition. But in absolutely every country on earth BICYCLES ARE PROHIBITED. Some of the placards add "and dogs," which for bicycles and dogs only increases their natural inferiority complexes twofold. A cat, a hare, a turtle, can in principle enter the import-export firm of Bunge & Born, or the lawyers' offices in the calle

San Martín, without occasioning more than surprise, captivating the overworked switchboard girls, or at worst, an order to the porter on the door to remove the aforementioned animals from the premises. This final alternative can certainly occur, but it is no humiliation, primarily because it constitutes only one probability among many, and secondly because it comes as a cause-and-effect situation and not as a coldly pre-established plot, a dreadfully perpetrated and general conspiracy printed on bronze plaques or enameled notices, inexorable tablets of the law which crush the simple spontaneity of bicycles, the innocent creatures.

Anyway, you managers, watch out! Roses are also ingenuous and tender, but perhaps you may know that in a war of roses princes died who were like black lightning, blinded by petals of blood. Might it not happen one day that the bicycles appear covered with thorns, that the shafts of their handlebars reverse themselves, grow like horns, and charge, that, armored with frenzy, they might not storm in legion the plate-glass windows of the insurance companies? And that unhappy day close with a general dip on the stock market, mourning dress prepared within twenty-four hours, and printed notes of acknowledgment for the sympathy cards, also printed.

THE BEHAVIOR OF MIRRORS
ON EASTER ISLAND

When you set up a mirror on the western side of Easter Island, it runs backwards. When you set one up on the eastern side of the island, it runs forward. Delicate surveys may discover the point at which that mirror will run on time, but finding the point at which that mirror works correctly is no guarantee that that point will serve for any other, since mirrors are subject to the defects of the individual substances of which they are made and react the way they really and truly want to. So that Solomon Lemos, an anthropologist on fellowship from the Guggenheim Foundation, looking into the mirror to shave, saw himself dead of typhus—this was on the eastern side of the island. And at the same time a tiny mirror which he'd forgotten on the western side of Easter Island (it'd been dropped between some stones) reflected for no one Solomon Lemos in short pants on his way to school, then Solomon Lemos naked in a bathtub being enthusiastically soaped by his mummy and daddy, then Solomon Lemos going da-da-da, to the thrilled delight of his Aunt Remeditos on a cattle ranch in Trenque Lanquen county.

THE POSSIBILITIES OF ABSTRACTION

I've been working for years at UNESCO and for other international organizations, in spite of which I manage to preserve some sense of humor and an especially noteworthy capacity for abstraction, which means for instance if I don't like a guy I wipe him, solely by deciding to do so, and while he talks and talks I've gone on to thinking about Melville and the poor guy thinks I'm listening. In the same way if there's a chick I like, she barely enters my field of vision and I can abstract the clothes off her, and while she talks to me about what a cold morning it is, I'm spending long minutes admiring her little belly button. This power that I have, sometimes it's almost unhealthy.

Last Monday it was ears. At the hour when everyone comes to work, it was extraordinary the number of ears whipping down the hall from the entrance. In my office I encountered six ears, in the cafeteria at noon there were over five hundred, symmetrically arranged in double rows. It was amusing from time to time to see a pair of ears rise, leave the assembly line, and move off. They looked like wings.

Julio Cortázar

I picked out something for Tuesday which I thought would be less ubiquitous—wrist watches. I was wrong, however, because at lunch I could see about two hundred of them hovering over the tables with a back-and-forth movement which reminded me particularly of the action of cutting up a beefsteak. Wednesday I preferred (with a certain embarrassment) something more fundamental, and I opted for buttons. What a show, wow! The air of the halls was filled with shoals of opaque eyes which crept horizontally, while alongside and somewhat below each little horizontal battalion, two, three, or four cuff buttons swung like pendulums. The saturation in the elevator was indescribable: hundreds of buttons, motionless or barely moving in an astonishing crystallographical cube. I remember one window especially (it was afternoon) against a blue sky. Eight red buttons sketched an exquisite vertical, and here and there a few small pearly secret disks moved delicately. She must have been a very beautiful woman.

It was Ash Wednesday, a day on which it seemed to me that the digestive processes would provide an adequate illustration of the event, so that at nine thirty I was the reluctant witness of the arrival of hundreds of guts full of a greyish pap as a result of the mixture of cornflakes, light coffee, and croissants. In the cafeteria I watched an orange being divided into triflingly neat sections which, at a given moment, lost their shape and descended one behind the other until at a certain height they formed a whitish deposit. In that state the orange hurried down the corridor, went down four floors, then, after entering an office, proceeded to immobilize itself at a point situated between the two arms of a chair. Somewhat further along you could see a quarter of a liter of strong tea in an analogous repose. As a curious parenthesis (my faculty for abstraction tends to exercise itself arbitrarily) you could see furthermore a puff of smoke that was descending vertically by a tube, split into two translucent bladders, ascend the tube again, and then with a pretty flourish disperse in its baroque consequences. Later (I was in another office), I found some pretext to go back and visit the orange, the tea, and the smoke. But the smoke had disappeared and in place of the orange and the tea there were two contorted tubes, rather disagreeable. Even abstraction has its distressing side; I said hello to the tubes and went back to my office. My secretary was crying, reading the memorandum informing me that they were letting me go. To console myself I decided to abstract her tears, and for a short time I took considerable pleasure in these diminutive crystalline fountains which appeared in the air and went plash on the bookshelves, the blotter, and the official bulletin. Life is full of such fair sights as these.

Julio Cortázar

THE DAILY DAILY

A man clambers onto the streetcar after having bought the daily paper and tucking it under his arm. Half an hour later he gets off, the same newspaper under the same arm.

Only now it's not the same newspaper, now it's a pile of printed sheets which the man drops on a bench in the plaza.

It hardly stays alone a minute on the bench, the pile of printed sheets is converted into a newspaper again when a young boy sees it, reads it, and leaves it converted into a pile of printed sheets.

It sits alone on the bench hardly a minute, the pile of printed sheets converts again into a newspaper when an old woman finds it, reads it, and leaves it changed into a pile of printed sheets. But then she carries it home and on the way home uses it to wrap up a pound of beets, which is what newspapers are fit for after all these exciting metamorphoses.

A SMALL STORY TENDING TO ILLUSTRATE THE UNCERTAINTY OF THE STABILITY WITHIN WHICH WE LIKE TO BELIEVE WE EXIST, OR LAWS COULD GIVE GROUND TO THE EXCEPTIONS, UNFORESEEN DISASTERS, OR IMPROBABILITIES, AND I WANT TO SEE YOU THERE

Confidential memo CVN/475 a/W
fr/ the Secretary of OCLUSIOM
to/ the Secretary of VERPERTUIT.

. . . terrible confusion. Everything was going beauti-
fully, no trouble ever with the regulations. Now suddenly
they decide to order a meeting of the Executive Committee in extraordinary session and the troubles begin, you'll
see what kind of messes turn up. Absolute confusion in
the ranks. Doubts as to the future. It happens that the
Committee meets and proceeds to elect new members to
replace the six office holders who fell under tragic circumstances, i.e., they fell into the water with the heli-
copter that was taking them on a survey of the desert
area, all of them perishing miserably in the regional

Julio Cortázar

hospital through a nurse mistakenly administering them sulfanilamide in doses clearly unacceptable to the human organism. The Committee meeting, consisting of the surviving Committee member (who'd had to stay home the day of the catastrophe because of a cold) and six alternate members, proceeds to vote on the candidates proposed by the different member-states that form Oclusiom. They elect unanimously Mr. Felix Voll (applause). They elect unanimously Mr. Felix Romero (applause). Another vote is called for, result, they unanimously elect Mr. Felix Lupescu (a certain uneasiness). The interim president takes the floor and makes a rather jocular allusion to the coincidence of first names. The Greek delegate requests the floor and declares that although it may seem somewhat peculiar, he has been instructed by his government to offer as candidate Mr. Felix Paparemologos. He is voted on and wins by a majority. The next vote comes up, and the Pakistani delegate, Mr. Felix Abib, carries it. At this point in the proceedings there is great confusion among the Committee, so it presses the final vote, with the result that the Argentine candidate, Mr. Felix Camusso, is elected. Amid the markedly uncomfortable applause of the present members, the senior Committee member welcomes the six new members, whom he qualifies cordially and designates as namesakes (stupefaction). The composition of the Committee is read and ends up organized in the following order: reading from the left, President and oldest surviving member, Mr. Felix Smith. Members: Felix Voll, Felix Romero, Felix Lupescu, Felix Paparemologos, Felix Abib, and Felix Camusso.

The election results put OCLUSIOM in true jeopardy at this point. The afternoon papers print the composition of the Executive Committee with jocular and impertinent comments. The Minister of the Interior spoke with the Director General this morning on the telephone. The latter, having nothing better at hand, had an informational memo prepared containing the *curriculum vitae* of the new Committee members, all of them eminent personalities in the field of the economic sciences.

The Committee must meet in its opening session this coming Thursday, but rumor has it that Mr. Felix Camusso, Mr. Felix Voll, and Mr. Felix Lupescu will send up their resignations this afternoon. Mr. Camusso has requested instructions as to how his resignation should be worded; in effect, he has no valid reason to offer for his resignation from the Committee, and as with Mr. Voll and Mr. Lupescu, his sole wish and sincerest advice is that the Committee be composed of gentlemen who do not answer to the name of Felix. The resignations, most probably, will cite reasons of health, and will be accepted by the Director General.

Julio Cortázar

END OF THE WORLD OF THE END

As the scribes will persist, the few readers there are in the world are going to have to change their roles and become scribes themselves. More and more countries will be made up of scribes, and more and more factories will be necessary to manufacture paper and ink, the scribes by day and the machines by night to print the scribes' work. First the libraries will overflow the houses, then the municipalities decide (now we're really into it) to sacrifice their children's playgrounds to enlarge the libraries. Then the theaters will go, then the maternity homes, slaughterhouses, bars, hospitals. The poor use the books like bricks, they stick them together with cement and build walls of books and live in cabins of books. Then it happens that the books clear the cities and invade the countryside, they go on flattening wheatfields and meadows of sunflowers, even though the Department of Highways manages to keep the roads cleared, even if only between two extremely high walls of books. At times a wall gives and there are terrifying automobile accidents. The scribes labor without let because humanity respects vocations, and the printed matter reaches the seashore. The President of the Republic gets on the telephone with the presidents of the republics, and intelligently proposes to cast the leftover books into the sea, which act is accomplished simultaneously on every coast in the world. Thus the Siberian scribes see their works cast into a sea of ice and the Indonesian scribes etc. This allows the scribes to step up their production as the earth again has space to store their books. It does not occur to them that the sea has a bottom and that at the bottom of the sea the printed matter is beginning to pile up, first in the form of a sticky pulp, then in the form of a solid pulp, and finally a tough though viscous flooring which rises several feet a day and will finally reach the surface. Then much of the water invades many of the lands and there is a new distribution of continents and oceans, and presidents of various republics are replaced by lakes and peninsulas, presidents of other republics see immense territories newly open to their ambitions, etc. Sea water, forced to expand with such unprecedented violence, evaporates faster than ever, or seeks rest, blending itself with the printed matter to make that glutinous pulp, to the point that one day ships' captains on the great trade routes report that their ships are advancing slowly, thirty knots drops to twenty, to fifteen, the engines sputter and pant and the propellers are wrenched and bent out of shape. Finally the ships stop wherever they are at different places in the sea, trapped by the pulp, and scribes all over the world write thousands of articles and books explaining the phenomenon and are filled with an enormous happiness. The presidents and the captains decide to convert the ships into islands and gambling casinos,

Julio Cortázar

the public arrives on foot upon the cardboard seas, and on these islands and casinos dance orchestras fill the night and sweeten the air-conditioned atmosphere and the dancing lasts until the early hours of the morning. New printed material is piling up on the seashores, but it's impossible to put it into the pulp, so that walls of printed matter are growing and mountains are being born on the shores of the old seas. The scribes realize that the ink and paper companies are going to go bankrupt, and their handwriting gets smaller and smaller and they use the most imperceptible corners of each sheet of paper. When the ink runs out they write in pencil, etc. When the paper goes, they write on slabs of wood or rock or on stone tiles, etc. The practice of intercalating one text into another begins to become popular, to take advantage of the space between the lines, or to scrape down the letters already printed with razor blades so as to use the paper again. The scribes are working slowly now, but their numbers are so immense that printed matter now separates the land completely from the beds of the ancient seas. On the earth the race of scribes lives precariously, doomed to extinction, and at sea there are the islands and casinos, or rather the ex-transatlantic liners, where the presidents of the republics have fled to refuge and where they hold enormous parties and exchange wireless messages from island to island, president to president, and captain to captain.

HEADLESSNESS

They cut off this gentleman's head, but as a strike broke out among the gravediggers and they couldn't bury him, the gentleman had to go on living headless and manage as well as he could.

He noticed immediately that, along with his head, four of his five senses had disappeared. Left solely with the sense of touch but full of good will, the gentleman seated himself on a bench in the plaza Lavalle and felt the leaves of the trees one by one, trying to distinguish them one from another and name them. Thus at the end of several days, he was reasonably sure that he had gathered and placed on his lap a eucalyptus leaf, one plantain, one wild magnolia, and a small green pebble.

When the gentleman observed that this latter item was a green pebble, he spent a very perplexed couple of days. Pebble was correct and maybe possible, but green, no. To test, he imagined the stone red and at the same moment felt a profound repugnance, a rejection of this flagrant falsehood, this absolutely false red pebble, for the pebble

Julio Cortázar

was completely green and disk-shaped, very sweet to the touch.

Furthermore, when he noticed that the stone was sweet, the gentleman was for a time subjected to great surprise. Then he opted for happiness, which is always preferable, since now he saw himself analogous to certain insects which can regenerate their amputated parts, he realized he was capable of feeling in divers ways. Stimulated by this conclusion, he left the bench in the plaza and went down via calle Libertad to the avenida de Mayo which, as everyone knows, is redolent of the smell of fried food from the Spanish restaurants. Confirming this detail, which gave him back another sense, the gentleman wandered vaguely west—or east—he couldn't be sure which, and he walked tirelessly, expecting from one moment to the next to be able to hear something, for now hearing was the one sense that he was still missing. What he was seeing actually was a sky, pallid as at dawn, he was touching his own hands with sweaty fingers, his fingernails pressing into the flesh of the palms, he smelled something like sweat, and in his mouth there was the taste of metal and cognac. The only sense lacking was hearing, and just then he heard, and it was like a memory, because what he again heard were the words of the prison chaplain, hopeful and consoling words by themselves, even very beautiful, but what a pity, they had that certain air of being used, said too many times, stale from having been said again and again.

ROUGH SKETCH OF A DREAM

He feels abruptly a great desire to see his uncle and hastens through the steep and twisting alleyways which seem to be straining to keep him away from the ancient mansion. After walking for a long time (and it's as though his feet were sticking to the ground) he sees the great gate and hears a dog bark in the distance, if that was a dog. As he is climbing the four worn-out steps and as he stretches out his hand toward the knocker, which is another hand grasping a bronze globe, the fingers of the knocker begin to move, the little finger first, then the others, which gradually let loose their grip on the bronze globe interminably. The globe falls as though it were made of feathers, rebounds noiselessly on the doorsill and leaps chest high, but now it is a fat black spider. He brushes it off with a desperate slap, and at that moment the door opens: his uncle is standing there smiling and expressionless, as though he had been standing there and waiting, smiling, behind the closed door for a long time. They exchange several sentences that seem to have been prepared, an elastic chess game. "Now I have to answer . . ." "Now he is going to say . . ." And

Julio Cortázar

everything happens exactly like that. Then they are in a brilliantly lit room, the uncle takes out some cigars wrapped in tinfoil and offers him one. He looks for the matches for a long time, but there are no matches or fire of any kind anywhere in the house; they cannot light the cigars, the uncle appears anxious that the visit end, and finally there is a confused leavetaking in a passageway filled with half-opened crates and where there's hardly room to move through.

Upon leaving the house, he knows that he ought not to look back *because* . . . He knows no more than that, but that he knows, and he leaves rapidly, his eyes fixed at the bottom of the street. Little by little he feels a bit more relieved. When he arrives home he is so exhausted that he lies down immediately, almost not bothering to undress. Then he dreams that he is in the Paraná Delta and that he passes the whole day rowing with his girlfriend and eating *chorizos* in the Nuevo Toro snack bar.

HOW'S IT GOING, LÓPEZ?

A gentleman meets a friend and greets him, shaking his hand and nodding a little.

Like that he thinks that he has said hello, but the greeting already exists and this good gentleman is only putting the greeting on for the umpteen-hundredth time.

It's raining. A gentleman takes shelter under an arcade. These gentlemen almost never know that they have just slid by prefabricated toboggan from the first rain to the first arcade. It is a wet toboggan of withered leaves.

And the gestures of love, that gentle museum, that gallery of figures of smoke. Let your vanity console itself: Mark Antony's hand sought what your hand seeks. And neither his nor yours was seeking anything that has not been found since eternity. But invisible things need to materialize themselves, ideas fall to earth like dead pigeons. The genuinely new creates either fear or wonderment. These two sensations equally close to the stomach always accompany the presence of Prometheus; the rest is convenience or profit, that which al-

Julio Cortázar

ways comes off more or less well; active verbs contain the whole repertory.

Hamlet has no doubt: he seeks the authentic solution, not the house door or the road already worn by whatever shortcut or crossroads proffer themselves. He wants the tangent that will smash the mystery into smithereens, the fifth leaf on the clover. Between yes and no what an infinite rose of the winds. The princes of Denmark, those falcons who elect to die of hunger before eating dead meat.

When the shoe pinches, it's a good sign. Something's happening here, something that shows us, that in a muffled way places and defines us. Which is the reason monsters are so popular and newspapers go into ecstasies over two-headed calves. What opportunities, what a prospect for a great leap toward otherness!

Here comes López.

"How's it going, López?"

"How's it going, buddy?"

And like that they think they have said hello.

GEOGRAPHIES

Established that ants are the true rulers of creation (the reader may take this as a hypothesis or as a fantasy; in any case he will do well with a little anthropoescapism), and I have here a page of their geography:

> (p. 84 of the book; possible equivalents of certain expressions are given in parentheses, following the classical interpretation of Gaston Loeb)

". . . parallel seas (rivers?). The infinite water (a sea?) grows at certain times like an ivy-ivy-ivy (idea of a very high wall, which would express the tides?). If one goes-goes-goes-goes (an analogous idea applied to distance) one comes to the Great Green Shade (a field under cultivation? a thicket? woods?) where the Great God raises up his perpetual granary for his Best Workers. Horrible Immense Beings (men?) abound in this region who destroy our trails under the earth. On the other side of the Great Green Shade, the Hard Sky begins (a mountain?). And all is ours, though under great threat."

Julio Cortázar

This geography has been the object of another interpretation (Dick Fry and Niels Peterson, Jr.). The landscape might correspond topographically to a small garden at 628 calle Laprida, Buenos Aires. The parallel seas are two gutters for waste water; the infinite water, a duck pond; the Great Green Shade, a bed of lettuce. The Horrible Immense Beings, they suggest, might be ducks or hens, though the possibility that, really, men are meant cannot be discarded. As for the Hard Sky, a polemic is already being waged which will not soon be resolved. In the opinion of Fry and Peterson, they hold it obvious that it means the brickyard next door, as opposed to the notion of Guillermo Sofovich, who surmises it to be a bidet abandoned among the lettuce.

PROGRESS AND RETROGRESSION

They invented a kind of glass which let flies through. The fly would come, push a little with his head and pop, he was on the other side. Enormous happiness on the part of the fly.

All this was ruined by a Hungarian scientist when he discovered that the fly could enter but not get out, or vice versa, because he didn't know what gimmick was involved in the glass or the flexibility of its fibers, for it was very fibroid. They immediately invented a fly trap with a sugar cube inside, and many flies perished miserably. So ended any possible brotherhood with these animals, who are deserving of better luck.

A VERY REAL STORY

It happened that a gentleman dropped his glasses on the floor, which, when they hit the tiles, made a terrible noise. The gentleman stoops down to pick them up, very dejected, as the lenses are very expensive, but he discovers with astonishment that by some miracle he hasn't broken them.

Now this gentleman feels profoundly thankful and understands that what has happened amounts to a friendly warning, in such a way that he walks down to an optician's shop and immediately acquires a leather glasses case, padded and double-protected, an ounce of prevention is worth a pound of, etc. An hour later the case falls, and stooping down to recover it without any great anxiety, he discovers that the glasses are in smithereens. It takes this gentleman a while to understand that the designs of Providence are inscrutable, and that in reality the miracle has just now occurred.

STORY WITH A SOFT BEAR

Now look at this ball of coal tar that oozes as it dilates, growing larger by the window juncture of two trees. Beyond the trees there's a clearing and it's there that the coal tar meditates and contemplates its entrance in the shape of a ball, the shape of a ball and paws, in the shape of coal tar   hair   paws   according to the dictionary BEAR.

Now the ball of coal tar emerges damp and soft shaking off infinite spherical ants, goes casting them off into each paw print which is disposed harmoniously as he walks. That is, the coal tar puts a bearpaw down upon the pine needles, fissuring the smooth earth and while pulling loose stamps a slipper in shreds forward and leaves newborn a multiple and rounded anthill, fragrant with coal tar. Thus on either side of the road, this founder of symmetrical realms walks, shaking off each damp pyramid of earth, a shape   hair   paws   contriving a structure for spherical ants.

At last the sun comes out and the soft bear raises a traveled and childlike face to the honeycomb he hungers for in vain. The coal tar begins to smell vehemently, the ball grows to the level of the day, hair paws only coal tar, hair paws coal tar that mumbles a plea and peers for the answer, the profound resounding of the honeycomb on high, honey of the sky on his tongue snout in his happiness hair paws.

THEME FOR A TAPESTRY

The general has only eighty men, and the enemy five thousand. In his tent the general curses and weeps. Then he writes an inspired proclamation and homing pigeons shower copies over the enemy camp. Two hundred foot desert to the general. There follows a skirmish which the general wins easily, and two regiments come over to his side. Three days later, the enemy has only eighty men and the general five thousand. Then the general writes another proclamation and seventy-nine men join up with him. Only one enemy is left, surrounded by the army of the general who waits in silence. The night passes and the enemy has not come over to his side. The general curses and weeps in his tent. At dawn the enemy slowly unsheathes his sword and advances on the general's tent. He goes in and looks at him. The army of the general disbands. The sun rises.

Julio Cortázar

PROPERTIES OF AN EASY CHAIR

At the Jacinto house there is an easy chair to die in. When people get old, one day they invite them to sit in the easy chair, which is a chair like any other but with a little silver star in the middle of the back. The invited person sighs, moves his hand a little as though he would like to hold the invitation at a distance, and then he goes and sits down in the chair and dies.

The boys, mischievous as always, amuse themselves in their mother's absence by playing tricks on visitors, and they invite them to sit in the chair. As the visitors are well informed but know that they must not talk about that, they look at the boys in great confusion and excuse themselves with words that are never used to talk to boys, which of course the boys find extremely hilarious. At the end the visitors avail themselves of any pretext to avoid sitting down, but later the boys' mother finds out what they've been up to and there are terrible beatings around bedtime. Not at all put off by this, every once in a while they succeed in tricking some innocent visitor and they have him sit in the chair. In these cases the parents cover up for them since they are afraid that the neighbors will discover the properties of the chair and will come over to ask the loan of it in order to get one or another of their family or circle of friends to sit down in it. Meanwhile the boys go on growing up and the day comes when, without knowing why, they lose interest in the chair and the visitors. They avoid even going into the parlor, they make a circuit around by the patio, and the parents, who are already very old, lock the parlor door with a key and look at their sons attentively as though wanting to-read-their-thoughts. The sons avoid the look and say that it's time to eat or time to go to sleep. Mornings, the father is the first one up and always goes to see if the parlor door is still locked, or if one of the sons has opened it so that the chair can be seen from the dining room, because the little silver star shines even in the darkness and it can be seen perfectly well from whatever part of the dining room.

Julio Cortázar

SCHOLAR WITH A HOLE
IN HIS MEMORY

Eminent scholar, Roman history in twenty-three volumes, sure candidate for Nobel prize, great enthusiasm in his country. Suddenly consternation: library creep and full-time hatchet man puts out scurrilous pamphlet denouncing omission of Caracalla. Relatively of little importance, but omission in any case. Stupefied admirers consult together Pax Romana which artist loses the world Varo return me my legions a man to all women and woman to all men (beware the Ides of March) money has no smell in this sign conquer. Incontrovertible evidence Caracalla missing, consternation, telephone disconnected, scholar cannot receive call from King Gustaf of Sweden, but that monarch is not even thinking of calling him, but rather another one who dials and dials the number in vain, cursing in a dead language.

PLAN FOR A POEM

Let Rome be the one that Faustina, let the wind sharpen the pencils of the seated scribe, or behind the hundred-year-old ivy let there appear written one morning this convincing sentence: there is no hundred-year-old ivy, botany is a science, to hell with the inventors of alleged images. And Marat in his bathtub.

I see as well the persecution of a cricket by a silver salver, with Lady Delia who brings her hand forward softly very like a noun and when it is about to trap the cricket it's in the salt (then they cross the Red Sea dry shod and Pharaoh damns them from the riverbank), or leaps up toward the delicate mechanism which extracts from the wheat flower the dry hand of toast. Lady Delia, Lady Delia, let that cricket go to wander through the flatware. One day he will sing with such terrible vengeance that your pendulum clocks will be strung up in their standing coffins, or the girl for the laundry will bring to light a living monogram which will run through the house repeating its initials like a tambourine player.

Julio Cortázar

Lady Delia, the guests are growing impatient because it's cold. And Marat in his bathtub.

Finally let it be Buenos Aires on a day sun up underway whirr like an arrow, with rags drying in the sun and every radio on the block blasting at the same time the price quotations on the free exchange for sunflowers. For a supernatural sunflower, the price in Liniers was eighty-eight pesos, and the sunflower made disgraceful statements to your Esso reporter, a little out of being tired after the recount of its seeds, in part because its ultimate fate did not figure in the ticket sale. In the afternoon there will be a concentration of labor forces in the plaza de Mayo. The forces will advance by different streets until they are counterpoised on the pyramid and it will be seen that they are laboring thanks to a system of reflexes installed by the municipality. No one doubts that the demonstrations will be acted out with the maximum brilliance, what has been provoked like is to suppose an extraordinary anticipation, the balconies will be packed. His Holiness the Cardinal will go, along with the doves, the imprisoned politicians, trolley conductors, watchmakers, the bribes, and the fat ladies. And Marat in his bathtub.

THE PRISONER

PRISONER. I'm not asking for much. A piece of bread, a
meat pie, a tiny light to hold between thumb
and middle finger. All I'd want would be a
box of matches so as to hear the rustling of
imprisoned ants that walk about inside. Even
if it were empty; I'm sure that if I held it
against my ear, I'd hear the rustling.

GUARD. Talking is not permitted except in French
or Italian.

PRISONER. A pity. Just the languages I left at home the
night I was arrested. They didn't leave me
time to put them on. Barely got into my un-
dershorts, and the official with the flushed
face started to kick me to make me hurry
up. They dragged me here, and the French
and the Italian were left behind, dumped into
some corner. I imagine they'll get hungry.
Do you think someone from the government
will give them something to eat?

GUARD. Don't know a thing.

PRISONER. Same as with insects, words go and come,
back and forth, getting paler and more ex-

Julio Cortázar

hausted all the time. First the conjunctions will die, their bodies are the weakest and the most easily replaceable.

GUARD. The conjunctions.

PRISONER. Then the adverbs and adjectives. The death of the adjectives is going to be very sad; like lights flickering out. Everyone knows that adjectives are the radiance of language.

GUARD. Death to the adjectives!

PRISONER. The verbs'll hold out to the end. And the nouns. Ah, they're not so easy. It's not just anybody can knock off a noun, figure it out. *Bread.* Who's going to kill that? And *Pine.* The axe hasn't been made can chop that down, no silence that'll hush its branches filled with small birds.

GUARD. Your imagination's feverish (*consults a manual*). You've got verbal mania, delirious association, and paralogism. Probably para-amnesia and fallacy of the generalities.

PRISONER. And am hungry. Very hungry.

GUARD. We'll kill you before long, then your hunger will pass.

PRISONER. I'll eat myself in delicate nibbles, a bit at a time.

GUARD. Of course you could always save yourself if you confess who has the plans to Operation H.

PRISONER. Of course I could always save myself if I confess who has the plans to Operation H.

GUARD. But . . .

PRISONER. Right.

CAMEL DECLARED UNDESIRABLE

They are accepting all petitions for entry across the
frontier but Guk, camel, unexpectedly declared undesirable. Guk applies to the Central Commissariat of Police,
they tell him nothing they can do, go back to the oasis,
declared an undesirable, useless to fill out petition. Guk's
sadness, his return to the land of his birth, and the
camels of his family and his friends gather around him,
and how did it go with you? and it's impossible, why you,
exactly? Then a delegation to the Minister of Transport
to present appeal in Guk's behalf, career functionaries
highly scandalized: something on this order never been
seen, you camels will return immediately to the oasis, a
brief will be drawn up.

Back at the oasis, Guk grazes one day, grazes another
day. All the camels have passed the frontier, Guk alone
still waits. This way summer passes, then autumn. Later
Guk goes back to the city, he stops in an empty plaza.
Much photographed by tourists according to newspaper
interviews. Vague prestige for Guk in the plaza. Seizing
the advantage he seeks to leave, at the gate everything

Julio Cortázar

changes: declared an undesirable. Guk's head droops, he takes up the sparse wisps of hay around the plaza. One day they call him on the loudspeaker and he comes happily into the prefecture. There he is declared undesirable. Guk returns to the oasis and lies down. He eats a little grass and later lays his muzzle on the sand. He is closing his eyes, meanwhile the sun is setting. From his nose there issues a bubble which lasts a second longer than he.

DISCOURSE OF THE BEAR

I'm the bear in the pipes of the house, I climb through the pipes in the hours of silence, the hot-water pipes, the radiator pipes, the air-conditioning ducts. I go through the pipes from apartment to apartment and I am the bear who goes through the pipes.

I think that they like me because it's my hair keeps the conduits clean, I run unceasingly through the tubes and nothing pleases me more than slipping through the pipes, running from floor to floor. Once in a while I stick my paw out through a faucet and the girl on the third floor screams that she's scalded herself, or I growl at oven height on the second, and Wilhelmina the cook complains that the chimney is drawing badly. At night I go quietly and it's when I'm moving most quickly that I raise myself to the roof by the chimney to see if the moon is dancing up there, and I let myself slide down like the wind to the boilers in the cellar. And in summer I swim at night in the cistern, prickled all over with stars, I wash my face first with one paw then with the other, finally with both together, and that gives me a great joy.

Julio Cortázar

Then I slide back down through the pipes of the house, growling happily, and the married couples stir in their beds and deplore the quality of the installation of the pipes. Some even put on the light and write a note to themselves to be sure to remember to complain when they see the superintendent. I look for the tap that's always running in some apartment and I stick my nose out and look into the darkness of rooms where those beings who cannot walk through the pipes live, and I'm always a little sorry for them, heavy beings, big ones, to hear how they snore and dream aloud and are so very much alone. When they wash their faces in the morning, I caress their cheeks and lick their noses and I leave, somewhat sure of having done some good.

PORTRAIT OF THE CASSOWARY

The first thing the cassowary does is to stare at one with a suspicious contempt. He restricts himself to looking without moving, staring in such a hard and continuous way that it's almost as though he were inventing us, as if by dint of terrifying strength he would extract us from the nothingness which is the cassowaries' world and set us down before him, in the inexplicable act of standing there looking at him.

From this double contemplation which may be single and perhaps basically no one, we are born, the cassowary and I, we settle down, we learn to disacknowledge one another. I don't know if the cassowary cuts me out and pastes me into its simple world; for my part I can only describe him, devote to his presence a chapter of likes and dislikes. Above all else, dislikes, because the cassowary is unlikable in the extreme and repulsive. Imagine an ostrich with a tea cosy of horn on his head, a bicycle smashed between two automobiles and which is piled up on itself, a decal which has taken poorly in which a dirty violet and a sort of crackling predominate.

.

Julio Cortázar

Now the cassowary takes a step forward and adopts a somewhat drier air; he is like a pair of spectacles surmounting an infinite pedantry. He lives in Australia, the cassowary; he is cowardly and fearsome at the same time; the guards enter his cage equipped with high leather boots and a flame thrower. When the cassowary stops his terrified running around the pan of bran they've put out for him and comes leaping at the keeper with great camel strides, there is no other recourse than to use the flame thrower. Then you see this: the river of fire envelops him and the cassowary, all his plumage ablaze, advances his last few steps bursting forth in an abominable screech. But his horn does not burn: the dry, scaly material which is his pride and his disdain goes into a cold melding, it catches fire with a prodigious blue, moving to a scarlet which resembles an excoriated fist, and finally congeals into the most transparent green, into an emerald, stone of shadow and of hope. The cassowary defoliates, a swift cloud of ash, and the keeper runs over greedily to possess the recently made gem. The zoo director always avails himself of this moment to institute proceedings against the keeper for the mistreatment of animals, and to dismiss him.

What more can we say of the cassowary, after this double misfortune?

FLATTENING THE DROPS

I don't know, look, it's terrible how it rains. It rains all the time, thick and grey outside, against the balcony here with big, hard, clabbering drops that go plaf and smash themselves like slaps, slop, one after the other, it's tedious. At the moment there's a little drop appears high on the window frame, and it stays there shivering against the sky which splits it into a thousand smothered glitterings, it goes on growing and totters, it's going to fall now, no it doesn't fall yet. It's hanging on by its nails, it doesn't want to fall and you can see that it's gripping hanging by its teeth meanwhile its belly is swelling it's a big drop already, what a fat one and suddenly whup, there it goes, plaf, effaced, nothing, a wetness on the marble.

But there are those that surrender and suicide immediately, they emerge on the window frame and hurl themselves down from there, it seems I can see the quaver of the leap, their little legs giving way and the cry that intoxicates them in that nothingness of falling and annihilation. Sad drops, rounded innocent drops. Goodbye drops. Goodbye.

Julio Cortázar

STORY WITH NO MORAL

A man sold cries and words, and he got along all right although he was always running into people who argued about his prices and demanded discounts. The man almost always gave in, and that way he was able to sell a lot of cries to street vendors, a few sighs which ladies on annuities usually bought, and words for fence posters, wall placards, slogans, letterheads, business cards, and used jokes.

The man realized finally that the hour had come and he requested an audience with the dictator of the country, who resembled all his colleagues and received him surrounded by generals, secretaries, and cups of coffee.

"I've come to sell you your last words," the man said. "They are very important because they'll never come out right for you when the moment comes, and on the other hand it would be suitable for you to say them at the critical moment so as in retrospect to shape easily an historical destiny."

"Translate what he's saying," the dictator ordered his interpreter.

"He's speaking Argentine, your Excellency."

"In Argentine? And how come I don't understand it?"

"You have understood very well," the man said. "I repeat, I've come to sell you your final words."

The dictator got to his feet as is the practice under these circumstances, and repressing a shiver ordered that they arrest the man and put him in the special dungeons which always exist in those administrative circles.

"It's a pity," said the man while they were leading him off. "In reality you would want to say your final words when the moment arrives, and it would be necessary to say them so as to shape in retrospect, and easily, an historical destiny. What I was going to sell you was what you yourself would want to say, so there's no cheating involved. But as you refuse to do business, you're not going to learn these words beforehand and when the moment arrives when they want to spring out for the first time, naturally you won't be able to say them."

"Why should I not be able to say them if they're what I would have wanted to say anyway?" demanded the dictator, already standing in front of another cup of coffee.

"Because fear will not let you," the man said sadly. "Since there will be a noose around your neck, you'll be in a shirt and shaking in terror and with the cold, your teeth chattering, and you won't be able to articulate a word. The hangman and his assistants, among whom there will be several of these gentlemen, will wait a

Julio Cortázar

couple of minutes for decorum's sake, but when your mouth brings forth only a moan interrupted by hiccups and appeals for a pardon (because that, sure, you'll articulate without trouble), they will come to the end of their patience and they'll hang you."

Highly indignant, the assistants and the generals in particular crowded around the dictator to beg that he have the fellow shot immediately. But the dictator, who was-pale-as-death, jostled all of them out the door and shut himself up with the man so as to buy his last words.

The generals and the secretaries in the meantime, humiliated in the extreme by the treatment they had received, plotted an uprising, and the following morning seized the dictator while he was eating grapes in his favorite pavilion. So that he should not be able to say his last words, they shot him then and there, eating grapes. Afterwards they set about to find the man, who had disappeared from the presidential palace, and it didn't take them long to find him since he was walking through the market selling routines to the comedians. Putting him in an armored car they carried him off to the fortress where they tortured him to make him reveal what the dictator's last words would have been. As they could not wring a confession from him, they killed him by kicking him to death.

The street vendors who had bought street cries went on crying them on streetcorners, and one of these cries served much later as the sacred writ and password for the counterrevolution which finished off the generals and the secretaries. Some of them, before their death, thought confusedly that really the whole thing had been a stupid chain of confusions, and that words and cries were things which, strictly speaking, could be sold but could not be bought, however absurd that would seem to be.

And they kept on rotting, the whole lot of them, the dictator, the man, and the generals and the secretaries, but from time to time on streetcorners, the cries could be heard.

Julio Cortázar

THE LINES OF THE HAND

From a letter thrown on the table a line comes which runs across the pine plank and descends by one of the legs. Just watch, you see that the line continues across the parquet floor, climbs the wall and enters a reproduction of a Boucher painting, sketches the shoulder of a woman reclining on a divan, and finally gets out of the room via the roof and climbs down the chain of lightning rods to the street. Here it is difficult to follow it because of the transit system, but by close attention you can catch it climbing the wheel of a bus parked at the corner, which carries it as far as the docks. It gets off there down the seam on the shiny nylon stocking of the blondest passenger, enters the hostile territory of the customs sheds, leaps and squirms and zigzags its way to the largest dock, and there (but it's difficult to see, only the rats follow it to clamber aboard) it climbs onto the ship with the engines rumbling, crosses the planks of the first-class deck, clears the major hatch with difficulty, and in a cabin where an unhappy man is drinking cognac and hears the parting whistle, it climbs the trouser seam, across the knitted vest, slips back to the elbow, and with a final push finds shelter in the palm of the right hand, which is just beginning to close around the butt of a revolver.

CRONOPIOS
AND FAMAS

I.

The First and Still Uncertain Appearance of Cronopios, Famas, and Esperanzas. Mythological Phase

NORMAL BEHAVIOR OF THE FAMAS

It happened that a fama was dancing respite and dancing catalan in front of a shop filled with cronopios and esperanzas. The esperanzas were the most irritated. They are always trying to see to it that the famas dance hopeful, not respite or catalan, since hopeful is the dance the cronopios and esperanzas know best.

The famas deliberately, always, locate directly in front of the shops, and at this time the fama was dancing respite and dancing catalan just to annoy the esperanzas. One of the esperanzas laid his flute fish on the floor—esperanzas, like the King of the Sea, are always accompanied by flute fishes—and went outside to curse at the fama, speaking to him like this:

—Fama, don't dance respite or catalan in front of this store.

The fama kept on dancing, and laughed.

The esperanza called out the other esperanzas, and the cronopios formed a circle around to see what would happen.

—Fama—said the esperanzas—don't dance respite or catalan either in front of this store.

But the fama kept on dancing and laughing to undermine the esperanzas.

Then the esperanzas hurled themselves upon the fama and wounded him. They left him lying beside a palisade, and the fama was lying there, lapped in his blood and gloom.

The cronopios, those wet green objects, came forward furtively and commiserated with him, speaking like this:

—Cronopio cronopio cronopio.

And the fama understood, and his solitude was less embittered.

DANCE OF THE FAMAS

The famas sing in a circle
the famas are singing and moving
about in a circle.

—CATALAN RESPITE RESPITE HOPEFUL

The famas are dancing in the room
with tiny lights and curtains
dance and sing in such a way that

—CATALAN RESPITE HOPEFUL RESPITE

O Park Department Employees,
how is it you let the famas get out, who walk freely
unrestrained, singing and dancing, the famas singing
catalan respite hopeful, how
can you?
If the cronopios (those green prickly humid things)
were still walking about the streets, one night
escape them with a greeting:—Gray day, cronopios
cronopios.
But the famas.

GAYETY OF THE CRONOPIO

An encounter between a cronopio and a fama at a liquidation sale in a shop called La Mondiale.

—Gray day, cronopio cronopio.

—Grade A, fama. Respite catalan hopeful.

—Cronopio cronopio?

—Cronopio cronopio.

—Thread?

—Two, but one blue one.

The fama considers the cronopio. He will not utter a sound until he's certain the words are precisely correct. Fearful that the always alert esperanzas, those sparkling microbes, will simply slip into the air, and through one mistaken word invade the cronopio's good-natured heart.

—Raining outside, the cronopio says.—The whole sky.

—Don't let it bother you, says the fama.—We'll go in my automobile. To keep the thread dry.

Julio Cortázar

He puts his head out the door and looks up and down the street. Not an esperanza in sight. He allows a sigh of satisfaction to escape. Furthermore, it pleases him to observe the touching gayety of the cronopio, who clutches against his chest the two threads—one blue one—and hopes anxiously that the fama is going to invite him to get into his car.

THE CRONOPIO BLUES

At the exit gate
to Luna Park a
cronopio notices that
his watch is running slow, that his watch is running
  slow, that his watch.

The cronopio has the blues
faced with a multitude of famas coming up calle Co-
  rrientes at twenty after two
while he, a damp green object, already leaving at two
  fifteen.
Cronopio's meditation: "It's late,
but not so late for me as for the famas, for the famas
it's five minutes later.
They'll arrive home later,
go to bed later. You know,
I've got a watch that's less lively, less homely, less going
  to bed when I go,

116   *Julio Cortázar*

I'm wet and unlucky.
I'm a cronopio."

While having a coffee in the Richmond Bar, the cronopio
dampens a piece of toast with his natural tears.

II.

Stories of
Cronopios and Famas

TRAVEL

When famas go on a trip, when they pass the night in a city, their procedure is the following: one fama goes to the hotel and prudently checks the prices, the quality of the sheets, and the color of the carpets. The second repairs to the commissariat of police and there fills out a record of the real and transferable property of all three of them, as well as an inventory of the contents of their valises. The third fama goes to the hospital and copies the lists of the doctors on emergency and their specialties.

After attending to these affairs diligently, the travelers join each other in the central plaza of the city, exchange observations, and go to a café to take an *apéritif*. But before they drink, they join hands and do a dance in a circle. This dance is known as "The Gayety of the Famas."

When cronopios go on a trip, they find that all the hotels are filled up, the trains have already left, it is raining buckets and taxis don't want to pick them up, either that or they charge them exorbitant prices. The cronopios are not disheartened because they believe firmly that these things happen to everyone. When they manage, finally, to find a bed and are ready to go to sleep, they say to one another, "What a beautiful city, what a very beautiful city!" And all night long they dream that huge parties are being given in the city and that they are invited. The next day they arise very contented, and that's how cronopios travel.

Esperanzas are sedentary. They let things and people slide by them. They're like statues one has to go visit. They never take the trouble.

Julio Cortázar

ON THE PRESERVATION
OF MEMORIES

To maintain the condition of their memories, the famas proceed in the following manner: after having fastened the memory with webs and reminders, with every possible precaution, they wrap it from head to foot in a black sheet and stand it against the parlor wall with a little label which reads: "EXCURSION TO QUILMES" or "FRANK SINATRA."

Cronopios, on the other hand, disordered and tepid beings that they are, leave memories loose about the house. They set them down with happy shouts and walk carelessly among them, and when one passes through running they caress it mildly and tell it, "Don't hurt yourself," and also "Be careful of the stairs." It is for this reason that the famas' houses are orderly and silent, while in those of the cronopios there is great uproar and doors slamming. Neighbors always complain about cronopios, and the famas shake their heads understandingly, and go and see if the tags are all in place.

CLOCKS

A fama had a wall clock, and each week he wound it VERY VERY CAREFULLY. A cronopio passed and noting this, he began to laugh, and went home and invented an artichoke clock, or rather a wild-artichoke clock, for it can and ought to be called both ways.

This cronopio's wild-artichoke clock is a wood artichoke of the larger species, fastened by its stem to a hole in the wall. Its innumerable leaves indicate what hour it is, all the hours in fact, in such a way that the cronopio has only to pluck a leaf to know what time it is. So he continues plucking them from left to right, always the leaf corresponds to that particular hour, and every day the cronopio begins pulling off a new layer of leaves. When he reaches the center, time cannot be measured, and in the infinite violet-rose of the artichoke heart the cronopio finds great contentment. Then he eats it with oil, vinegar, and salt and puts another clock in the hole.

Julio Cortázar

THE LUNCH

Not without some labor, a cronopio managed to invent a thermometer for measuring lives. Something between a thermograph and a topometer, between a filing cabinet and a *curriculum vitae*.

For example, the cronopio received at his house a fama, an esperanza, and a professor of languages. Applying his discoveries, he established that the fama was infra-life, the esperanza para-life, and the professor of languages inter-life. As far as the cronopio himself was concerned, he considered himself just slightly super-life, but more poetry in that than truth.

Came lunchtime, this cronopio took great pleasure in the conversation of his fellow members, because all of them thought they were referring to the same things, which was not so. The inter-life was maneuvering such abstractions as spirit and conscience, to which the para-life listened like someone hearing rain—a delicate job. Naturally, the infra-life was asking constantly for the grated cheese, and the super-life carved the chicken in forty-two separate movements, the Stanley Fitzsimmons method. After dessert, the lives took their leaves of one another and went off to their occupations, and there was left on the table only little loose bits of death.

Julio Cortázar

HANDKERCHIEFS

A fama is very rich and has a maid. When this fama finishes using a handkerchief, he throws it in the wastepaper basket. He uses another and throws it in the basket. He goes on throwing all the used handkerchiefs into the basket. When he's out of them, he buys another box.

The servant collects all the handkerchiefs and keeps them for herself. Because she is so surprised at the fama's conduct, one day she can no longer contain herself and asks if, really and truly, the handkerchiefs are to be thrown away.

—Stupid idiot, says the fama—*you shouldn't have asked*. From now on you'll wash my handkerchiefs and I'll save money.

BUSINESS

The famas had opened a factory to make garden hoses and had employed a large number of cronopios to coil and store them in the warehouse.

The cronopios were hardly in the building where the hoses were manufactured—an incredible gayety! There were green hoses, blue hoses, yellow hoses, and violet hoses. They were transparent and during the testing you could see water running through them with all its bubbles and occasionally a surprised insect. The cronopios began to emit shouts and wanted to dance respite and dance catalan instead of working. The famas grew furious and applied immediately articles 21, 22, and 23 of the internal regulations. In order to avoid the repetition of such goings-on.

As the famas are very inattentive, the cronopios hoped for *favorable circumstances* and loaded very many hoses into a truck. When they came across a little girl, they cut a piece of blue hose and gave it to her as a present so that she could jump rope with it. Thus on all the streetcorners there appeared very lovely, blue, transparent bubbles with a little girl inside, who seemed to be a squirrel in a treadmill. The girl's parents had aspirations: they wanted to take the hose away from her to water the garden, but it was known that the astute cronopios had punctured them in such a way that the water in them broke all into pieces and would serve for nothing. At the end, the parents got tired and the girl went back to the corner and jumped and jumped.

The cronopios decorated divers monuments with the yellow hoses, and with the green hoses they set traps in the African fashion, right in the middle of the rose park, to see how the esperanzas would fall into them one by one. The cronopios danced respite and danced catalan around the trapped esperanzas, and the esperanzas reproached them for the way they acted, speaking like this:

—Bloody cronopios. Cruel, bloody cronopios!

The cronopios, who had no evil intentions toward the esperanzas, helped them get up and made them gifts of sections of red hose. In this way, the esperanzas were able to return home and accomplish their most intense desire: to water green gardens with red hoses.

The famas closed down the factory and gave a banquet replete with funereal speeches and waiters who served the fish with great sighs. And they did not invite one cronopio, and asked only those esperanzas who hadn't fallen into the traps in the rose gardens, for the others were still in possession of sections of hose and the famas were angry with these particular esperanzas.

PHILANTHROPY

Famas are capable of gestures of great generosity. For example: this fama comes across a poor esperanza who has fallen at the foot of a coconut palm. He lifts him into his car, takes him home, and busies himself with feeding him and offering him diversion until the esperanza has regained sufficient strength, and tries once more to climb the coconut palm. The fama feels very fine after this gesture, and really he is very goodhearted, only it never occurs to him that within a few days the esperanza is going to fall out of the coconut palm again. So, while the esperanza has fallen once more to the foot of the coconut palm, the fama, at his club, feels wonderful and thinks about how he helped the poor esperanza he found lying there.

Cronopios are not generous on principle. They pass to one side of the most touching sights, like that of a poor esperanza who does not know how to tie his shoe and whimpers, sitting on the sidewalk by the curb. These cronopios do not even look at the esperanza, being completely occupied with staring at some floating dandelion

Julio Cortázar

fuzz. With beings like that, beneficence cannot be prac-
ticed coherently. For which reason the heads of philan-
thropic societies are all famas, and the librarian is an
esperanza. From their lofty positions the famas help the
cronopios a lot, but the cronopios don't fret themselves
over it.

THE PUBLIC HIGHWAYS

A poor cronopio is driving along in his automobile. He comes to an intersection, the brakes fail, and he smashes into another car. A traffic policeman approaches, terribly, and pulls out a little book with a blue cover.

—Don't you know how to drive? the cop shouts.

The cronopio looks at him for a moment and then asks:

—Who are you?

The cop remains grim and immovable, but glances down at his uniform, as though to convince himself that there's been no mistake.

—Whaddya mean, who am I? Don't you see who I am?

—I see a traffic policeman's uniform, explains the cronopio, very miserable.—You are inside the uniform, but the uniform doesn't tell me who you are.

The policeman raises his hand to give him a hit, but then he has the little book in one hand and the pencil in the

Julio Cortázar

other, in such a way that he doesn't hit the cronopio, but goes to the front of the automobile to take down the license-plate number. The cronopio is very miserable and regrets having gotten into the accident because now they will continue asking him questions and he will not be able to answer them, not knowing who is doing the asking, and among strangers there can be no understanding.

SONG OF THE CRONOPIOS

When the cronopios sing their favorite songs, they get so excited, and in such a way, that with frequency they get run over by trucks and cyclists, fall out of windows, and lose what they're carrying in their pockets, even losing track of what day it is.

When a cronopio sings, the esperanzas and famas gather around to hear him, although they do not understand his ecstasy very well and in general show themselves somewhat scandalized. In the center of a ring of spectators, the cronopio raises his little arms as though he were holding up the sun, as if the sky were a tray and the sun the head of John the Baptist, in such a way that the cronopio's song is Salome stripped, dancing for the famas and esperanzas who stand there agape asking themselves if the good father would, if decorum. But because they are good at heart (the famas are good and the esperanzas are blockheads), they end by applauding the cronopio, who recovers, somewhat startled, looks around, and also starts to applaud, poor fellow.

Julio Cortázar

STORY

A small cronopio was looking for the key to the street
door on the night table, the night table in the bedroom,
the bedroom in the house, the house in the street. Here
the cronopio paused, for to go into the street, he needed
the key to the door.

THE NARROW SPOONFUL

A fama discovered that virtue was a spherical microbe with a lot of feet. Immediately he gave a large table-spoonful to his mother-in-law. The result was ghastly: the lady ceased and desisted from her sarcastic comments, founded a club for lost Alpine climbers, and in less than two months conducted herself in such an exemplary manner that her daughter's defects, having up till then passed unnoticed, came with great suddenness to the first level of consideration, much to the fama's stupefaction. There was no other recourse than to give a spoonful of virtue to his wife, who abandoned him the same night, finding him coarse, insignificant, and all in all, different from those moral archetypes who floated glittering before her eyes.

The fama thought for a long while and finally swallowed a whole flask of virtue. But all the same, he continued to live alone and sad. When he met his mother-in-law or his wife in the street, they would greet one another respectfully and from afar. They did not even dare to speak to one another. Such was his perfection and their fear of being contaminated.

Julio Cortázar

THE PHOTO CAME OUT BLURRED

A cronopio is about to open the door to the street, and upon putting his hand in his pocket to take out the key, what he emerges with is a box of matches, whereupon this cronopio grows extremely upset and begins to think that if, in place of the key, he finds matches, it would be horrible if at one stroke the world were to be transposed, and at best, if the matches were where the key should have been, why shouldn't it happen that he would find his wallet full of matches, the sugar bowl full of money, and the piano full of sugar, and the telephone directory full of music, the wardrobe full of commuters, the bed full of men's suits, the flowerboxes full of sheets, the trams full of roses, and the countryside full of trams. So it happens that this cronopio is horribly dejected and runs to look at himself in the mirror, but as the mirror is somewhat tilted, what he sees is the umbrella stand in the vestibule and his worst suspicions are confirmed. He snaps. He breaks into sobs, he falls to his knees and wrings his little hands and doesn't know why. The famas who are neighbors of his gather around to console him, and the esperanzas also. But hours pass before the cronopio can emerge from his despair and accept a cup of tea, which he looks at and examines thoroughly before drinking, whether instead of a glass of tea it might not be an anthill or a book of Samuel Smiles.

EUGENICS

It happens that cronopios do not want to have sons, for the first thing a recently born cronopio does is to be grossly insulting to his father, in whom he sees obscurely the accumulation of misfortunes that will one day be his own.

Given these reasons, the cronopios turn to the famas for help in fecundating their wives, a situation toward which the famas are always well disposed, it being a question of libidinous character. They believe furthermore that in this way they will be undermining the moral superiority of the cronopios, but in this they are stupidly mistaken, for the cronopios educate their sons in their own fashion and within a few weeks have removed any resemblance to the famas.

HIS FAITH IN THE SCIENCES

An esperanza believed in physiognomical types, such as for instance the pugnosed type, the fish-faced type, those with a large air intake, the jaundiced type, the beetle-browed, those with an intellectual face, the hairdresser type, etc. Ready to classify these groups definitively, he began by making long lists of acquaintances and dividing them into the categories cited above.

He took the first group, consisting of eight pugnosed types, and noticed that surprisingly these boys divided actually into three subgroups, namely pugnoses of the mustached type, pugnoses of the pugilist type, and pugnoses of the ministry-appointee sort, composed respectively of 3, 3, and 2 pugnoses in each particularized category. Hardly had he separated them into their new groupings (at the Paulista Bar in the calle San Martín, where he had gathered them together at great pains and no small amount of coffee with sweet cream, well whipped) when he noticed that the first subgroup was not homogenous, since two of the mustached-type pugnoses belonged to the rodent variety while the remaining

Julio Cortázar

one was most certainly a pugnose of the Japanese-court sort. Well. Putting this latter one aside, with the help of a hefty sandwich of anchovies and hard-boiled eggs, he organized a subgroup of the two rodent types, and was getting ready to set it down in his notebook of scientific data when one rodent type looked to one side and the other turned in the opposite direction, with the result that the esperanza, and furthermore everyone there, could perceive quite clearly that, while the first of the rodent types was evidently a brachycephalic pugnose, the other exhibited a cranium much more suited to hanging a hat on than to wearing one.

So it was that the subgroup dissolved, and as for the rest, better not to mention it, since the remainder of the subjects had graduated from coffee with sweet cream to coffee with flaming cognac, and the only way in which they seemed to resemble one another at the height of these festivities was in their common and well-entrenched desire to continue getting drunk at the expense of the esperanza.

NEVER STOP THE PRESSES

A fama was working so hard in the raw-tea industry that he didn't-have-time-for-anything. Thus this fama languished at odd moments, and raising-his-eyes-to-heaven, frequently cried out:

—How I suffer! I'm a victim of my work, notwithstanding being an example of industry and assiduity, my-life-is-a-martyrdom!

Touched and depressed by his employer's anxiety, an esperanza who was working as a typist in the accounting office of the fama got up enough nerve to address himself to the fama, speaking like this:

—Gray day, fama fama. If you solitary occasion work, I pull solution right away from left pocket.

The fama, with the amiability characteristic of his class, knitted his eyebrows and extended his hand. A miracle! Among his fingers, there the world lay caught, and the fama had no reason to complain of his luck. Every morning the esperanza came in with a fresh supply of

Julio Cortázar

miracle and the fama, installed in his armchair, would receive a declaration of war and/or a declaration of peace, or a selected view of the Tyrol and/or of Bariloche and/or of Porto Alegre, the latest thing in motors, a lecture, a photo of an actress and/or of an actor, etc. All of which cost him only a dime, which is not very much bread if you're buying the world.

IMPROPRIETIES IN THE PUBLIC SERVICE

See what happens when you trust the cronopios. Hardly had he been named Director General of Radio Diffusion when this cronopio called in several translators from the calle San Martín, and had them translate all the scripts, commercials, and songs into Rumanian, a language not very popular in Argentina.

At eight in the morning the famas began to tune in their receivers, wishing to hear the news bulletins as well as the commercials for GENITAL, the Cigarette with Sex, and for COOK's OIL, the Kitchen Oil That WON'T Soil.

And they heard them, but in Rumanian, so that they understood only the trade name of the product. Profoundly astonished, the famas shook and beat on their radios, but everything rumbled on in Rumanian including the tango *I'm Getting Drunk Tonight,* and the telephone at the Radio Diffusion Center was tended by a young lady who answered the loud and numerous complaints in Rumanian, which imparted a certain warmth to the confusion daddy.

Advised of the situation, the Administration gave the order to shoot the cronopio who had so besmirched the traditions of his native land. Through a mischance, the firing squad was composed of conscript cronopios who, instead of firing on the ex-Director General, fired over the crowd in the plaza de Mayo with such excellent aim that they bagged six naval officers and a pharmacist. A firing squad of famas turned out, the cronopio was duly executed, and a distinguished author of folksongs and of an essay on gray matter was designated to take his place. This fama re-established Spanish as the language on the Radio Diffusion, but it happened so that the famas had already lost their confidence and hardly ever turned their radios on. Many famas, pessimists by nature, had bought manuals and dictionaries in Rumanian, as well as biographics of King Carol and Magda Lupescu. Rumanian came into fashion despite the Administration's indignation, and delegations made furtive pilgrimages to the cronopio's tomb, where they let fall their tears and calling cards, cards teeming with names well known in Bucharest, a city with many stamp collectors and assassins.

MAKE YOURSELF AT HOME

An esperanza built a house and plastered up a tile which read:

> WELCOME ALL
> WHO COME TO THIS HOME

A fama built a house and did not put up a tile in the first place.

A cronopio built a house and, following the custom, set into the porch divers tiles which he bought or had made. The tiles were cemented up in such a way that they could be read in order. The first said:

> WELCOME ALL
> WHO ENTER THIS HOME

The second said:

> THE HOUSE IS SMALL
> BUT THE HEART IS IMMENSE

The third:

> THE PRESENCE OF A GUEST
> IS AS SOFT AS REST

Julio Cortázar

The fourth:

> WE ARE POOR BUT STILL
> WE HAVE GOOD WILL

And the fifth read:

> THIS ORDINANCE CANCELS ALL PREVIOUS ANNOUNCEMENTS
> BEAT IT!

THERAPIES

A cronopio receives his medical degree and opens a practice in the calle Santiago del Estero. A patient arrives almost immediately and tells him how there are places that ache and how there are places that ache and how he doesn't sleep at night and eats nothing during the day.

—Buy a large bouquet of roses, the cronopio tells him.

The patient leaves, somewhat surprised, but he buys the bouquet and is instantly cured. Bursting with gratitude, he returns to the cronopio and not only pays him but, as a delicate testimonial, he presents him with the gift of a handsome bouquet of roses. He has hardly left the office when the cronopio falls ill, aches all over, can't sleep at night, and eats nothing during the day.

Julio Cortázar

THE PARTICULAR AND THE UNIVERSAL

A cronopio was about to brush his teeth standing next to his balcony, and being possessed by a very incredible gayety to see the morning sun and the handsome clouds racing through the sky, he squeezed the tube of toothpaste prodigiously and the toothpaste began to emerge in a long pink strip. After having covered his brush with a veritable mountain of toothpaste, the cronopio found he had some left over, started to flap the tube out the window still squeezing away and strips of pink toothpaste fell over the balcony into the street where several famas had gathered to discuss municipal scandals. The strips of pink toothpaste landed all over the famas' hats, while up above, the cronopio was singing away and filled with great contentment was brushing his teeth. The famas grew very indignant over this incredible lack of self-consciousness on the cronopio's part, and decided to appoint a delegation to upbraid him immediately. With which the delegation, composed of three famas, tromped up the stairs to the cronopio's apartment and reproached him, addressing him like this:

—Cronopio, you've ruined our hats, you'll have to pay for them.

And afterward, with a great deal more force:

—Cronopio, you shouldn't have wasted your toothpaste like that!

THE EXPLORERS

Three cronopios and a fama join forces, speleologically speaking, in order to discover the subterranean sources of a spring. Arriving at the cavern's mouth, one cronopio descends supported by the others, carrying at one shoulder a package containing his favorite sandwiches (cheese). The two cronopio assistants lower him little by little, and the fama writes the details of the expedition down in a large notebook.

The first message from the cronopio soon arrives: "Furious. You have made primary error. Have included only ham sandwiches." He shakes the rope and demands that they pull him up.

The two cronopio assistants consult with one another miserably, and the fama draws himself up to his most terrible stature and says NO! with such violence that the cronopios let go of the rope and run over to calm him.

They are occupied with this when another message arrives, for the cronopio it seems has fallen exactly on top of the source of the spring, and from that vantage point communicates that everything is going badly, and informs them between insults and tears that the sandwiches are all ham, and no matter how he looks and looks, that among all those ham sandwiches there is not even one of cheese.

EDUCATION OF THE PRINCE

Cronopios hardly ever have sons, but when they do have them they lose their heads and extraordinary things occur. For example, a cronopio has a son, and immediately afterward wonderment invades him, and he is certain that his son is the very peak and summit of beauty and that all of chemistry runs through his veins with here and there islands of fine arts, poetry, and urban architecture. Then it follows that this cronopio cannot even look at his son but he bows deeply before him and utters words of respectful homage.

The son, as is natural, hates him fastidiously.

When he comes of school age, his father registers him in 1-B, and the child is happy with other little cronopios, famas, and esperanzas. But he knows that when class is out his father will be waiting for him and upon seeing him will raise his hands and say divers thing, such as:

—Grade A, cronopio cronopio, tallest and best and most rosy-cheeked and most particular and most dutiful and most diligent of sons!

Whereat the junior famas and junior esperanzas are doubled up with laughter at the street curb, and the small cronopio hates his father with great pertinacity and consistency and will always end by playing him a dirty trick somewhere between first communion and military service. But the cronopios do not suffer too much from this, because they also used to hate their fathers, to such point as it seems likely that this hate is the other name for liberty or for the immense world.

Julio Cortázar

PLACE THE STAMP IN THE UPPER
RIGHT-HAND CORNER OF THE
ENVELOPE

A fama and a cronopio are very good friends and go together to the post office to mail several letters to their wives who are traveling in Norway, thanks to the diligence of Thos. Cook & Sons.

The fama sticks his stamps on with prolixity, beating on them lightly numerous times so that they will stick well, but the cronopio lets go with a terrible cry, frightening the employees, and with immense anger declares that the portraits on the stamps are repugnant and in bad taste and that never shall he be obliged to prostitute his love letters to his wife with such sad pieces of work as these. The fama feels highly uncomfortable because he has already stamped his letters, but as he is a very good friend of the cronopio, he would like to maintain solidarity with him and ventures to say that in fact, the twenty-centavo stamp is vulgar in the extreme and repetitious, but that the one-peso stamp has the fuzzy color of settling wine.

None of this calms the cronopio, who waves his letter and exhorts, apostrophizes, and declaims at the employees, who gaze at him completely stupefied. The postmaster emerges and hardly twenty seconds later the cronopio is in the street, letter in hand, and burdened with a great sorrow. The fama, who has furtively posted his in the drop box, turns to consoling him and says:

—Luckily our wives are traveling together, and in my letter I said that you were all right, so that your wife can read it over my wife's shoulder.

TELEGRAMS

An esperanza exchanged the following telegrams with her sister, between the suburb of Ramos Mejía and Viedma:

YOU FORGOT CANARY'S CUTTLEBONE. STUPID. INÉS.

STUPID YOURSELF. I HAVE REPLACEMENT. EMMA.

Three telegrams from cronopios:

UNEXPECTEDLY I MISTOOK THE TRAIN IN PLACE OF THE 7:12 I TOOK THE 8:24 AM IN A CRAZY PLACE. SINISTER MEN COUNT POSTAGE STAMPS. HIGHLY LUGUBRIOUS LOCATION. DON'T THINK THEY'LL LET THE TELEGRAM THROUGH. WILL LIKELY FALL SICK. TOLD YOU I SHOULD HAVE BROUGHT HOT-WATER BOTTLE. VERY DEPRESSED SITTING STAIRWAY WAITING TRAIN BACK. ARTURO.

NO. FOUR PESOS SIXTY OR NOTHING. IF THEY GIVE THEM TO YOU FOR LESS BUY TWO PAIRS, ONE PLAIN THE OTHER WITH STRIPES.

FOUND AUNT ESTHER CRYING, TURTLE SICK. POISONOUS ROOT IT SEEMS OR CHEESE TERRIBLE CONDITIONS. TURTLES DELICATE ANIMALS. SOMEWHAT STUPID, DON'T DISCRIMINATE. A SHAME.

Lion and Cronopio

A cronopio who was crossing the desert encountered a lion, and the following dialogue took place:

LION.   I eat you.

CRONOPIO (*terribly worried but with dignity*).   Okay.

LION.   Ah, none of that. None of this martyrdom with me. Lie down and cry, or fight, one of the two. I can't eat you like that. Let's go, I'm waiting. Say something.

The cronopio says nothing, and the lion is perplexed; finally an idea comes to him.

LION.   Damn the luck, I have in my left paw a thorn that annoys me exceedingly. Take it out for me and I'll let you go.

The cronopio removes the thorn and the lion goes off snarling in a poor temper:

—Thanks, Androcles.

Julio Cortázar

Condor and Cronopio

A condor fell like a streak of lightning upon a cronopio who was passing through Tinogasta, corralled him against a concrete wall, and in high dudgeon addressed him, like for instance:

CONDOR.   Dare you to say I'm not handsome.

CRONOPIO.   You're the handsomest bird I've ever seen.

CONDOR.   Again, more.

CRONOPIO.   You are more handsome than a bird of paradise.

CONDOR.   I dare you to say I don't fly high.

CRONOPIO.   You fly to the most dizzying heights and you are completely supersonic and stratospheric.

CONDOR.   Dare you to say I stink.

CRONOPIO.   You smell better than a whole liter of Jean-Marie Farina cologne.

CONDOR.   What a shitheel you are. Not leaving the vaguest possibility of taking even a peck at you.

Flower and Cronopio

A cronopio runs across a solitary flower in the middle of
the fields. At first he's about to pull it up,
    but then he thinks,
    this is a useless cruelty,
    and he gets down on his knees beside it
and plays lightheartedly with the flower, to see he
caresses the petals, he puffs at it until it dances, he
buzzes at it like a bee, he inhales its perfume, and finally
he lies down under the flower and falls asleep, enveloped
in a profound peace.

The flower thinks: "He's like a flower."

Fama and Eucalyptus

A fama is walking through a forest, and although he
needs no wood he gazes greedily at the trees. The trees
are terribly afraid because they are acquainted with the
customs of the famas and anticipate the worst. Dead
center of the wood there stands a handsome eucalyptus
and the fama on seeing it gives a cry of happiness and

dances respite and dances catalan around the disturbed eucalyptus, talking like this:

—Antiseptic leaves, winter with health, great sanitation!

He fetches an axe and whacks the eucalyptus in the stomach. It doesn't bother the fama at all. The eucalyptus screams, wounded to death, and the other trees hear him say between sighs:

—To think that all this imbecile had to do was buy some Valda tablets.

Turtles and Cronopios

Now it happens that turtles are great speed enthusiasts, which is natural.

The esperanzas know that and don't bother about it.

The famas know it, and make fun of it.

The cronopios know it, and each time they meet a turtle, they haul out the box of colored chalks, and on the rounded blackboard of the turtle's shell they draw a swallow.

Julio Cortázar, an Argentine who was born in Brussels in 1914, has lived and worked in Paris since 1952. He is a poet, translator, and amateur jazz musician as well as the author of several volumes of short stories and novels. Pantheon has published seven of his books in English: *The Winners*, *Hopscotch*, *End of the Game*, *Cronopios and Famas*, *62: A Model Kit*, *All Fires the Fire*, and *A Manual for Manuel*.